AUSTRALIA'S
CONVICT PAST

AUSTRALIA'S
CONVICT PAST

ROBERT COUPE

NEW HOLLAND

First published in Australia in 2002 by
New Holland Publishers (Australia) Pty Ltd
Sydney • Auckland • London • Cape Town

14 Aquatic Drive Frenchs Forest NSW 2086 Australia
218 Lake Road Northcote Auckland New Zealand
86 Edgware Road London W2 2EA United Kingdom
80 McKenzie Street Cape Town 8001 South Africa

National Library of Australia Cataloguing-in-Publication Data:

Coupe, Robert.
Australia's convict past
Includes index.
ISBN 1 86436 707 5.

1. Convicts – Australia – History. 2. Penal colonies. 3. Australia – History – 1788-1851. I. Title.

994.02

Publishing Manager: Anouska Good
Editor and picture researcher: Sophie Church
Designer: Nanette Backhouse
Design concept: Patricia McCallum
Cartographer: Ian Faulkner
Production Controller: Wendy Hunt
Reproduction: Pica Digital, Singapore
Printer: Kyodo Printing, Singapore

10 9 8 7 6 5 4 3 2 1

Picture acknowledgements

By permission of the Allport Library and Museum of Fine Arts, State Library of Tasmania: p.51, Thomas Lempriere, *Grummet Island off Sarah Island*.

By permission of the Archives Office of Tasmania: p.51, *Matthew Brady*, ref. 52/4/1; **p.61**, plans of Cascades Female Factory.

Courtesy Battye Library: p.63, Government House, Perth, ref. 21465P.

By permission of the British Library: p. 22, William Jackson, *The Convicts taking water near Blackfriars Bridge in order for their being conveyed to Woolwich*, shelfmark 1132.f54–59; **p.23**, J.P. Andrews, *An appeal to the humane on behalf of the climbing boys*, shelfmark 104.k.

By permission of Coo-ee Historical Picture Library: p.31, David Wilkie, *The Breakfast*.

By permission of the National Library of Australia: front cover and p.46, Augustus Earle, *A Government Jail Gang*; **back cover and p.53**, G.C. Mundy, *Convict Tramway*; **pp.3 and 14**, Thomas Rowlandson, *Convicts Embarking at Botany Bay*; **pp.5 and 9**, Edward William Cooke, *Prison-ship in Portsmouth Harbour*; **p.6**, F. Wheatley, *Arthur Phillip*; **p.8**, Public hanging, frontispiece to *Life and Death of John Carpenter*; **p.10**, Captain James Cook, copy of an original by Nathaniel Dance; **p.11**, M. MacLeod, *Natives Opposing Captain Cook's Landing*; **p.12**, Sir Joseph Banks; **p.13**, Thomas Luny, *The Bark Earl of Pembroke, later Endeavour, leaving Whitby Harbour*; **p.15**, George Raper, *View of the Island of Teneriffe* [sic]; **p.17**, George Raper, *Entrance of Rio de Janeiro from the anchorage without the Sugar Loaf*; **p.20**, *Captain Phillip's First Sight of Port Jackson*; **p.24**, George Raper, *The Melancholy Loss of HMS Sirius off Norfolk Island 19 March 1790*; **p.27**, Joseph Lycett, *Aborigines Spearing Fish, Others Diving for Crayfish, a Party Seated Beside a Fire Cooking Fish*; **p.28**, *Early Government House Sydney*; **p.29**, Francis Fowkes, *Sketch & Description of the Settlement at Sydney Cove in the County of Cumberland 1789*; **p.30**, James Heath, *A View of the Governor's House at Rosehill, in the Township of Parramatta 1798*; **p.32**, John Eyre, *Sydney Cove, East Side*; **p.33**, *Black-eyed Sue and Sweet Poll of Plymouth Taking Leave of their Lovers who are Going to Botany Bay*; **p.35**, Isaac Cruikshank, *The Soldiers Farewell, Soldiers Embarking for New South Wales*; **p.36**, Jean Francois Galaup, *Comte De La Perouse*; **p.37**, *Governor Philip Gidley King*; **p.38**, Edward Dayes, *View of Sydney on the South Side of Norfolk Island*; **p.40**, *Arrest of Governor Bligh*; Alexander Huey, *Portrait of Rear Admiral William Bligh*; **p.42**, Joseph Lycett, *The residence of John McArthur Esq. Near Parramatta New South Wales*; **p.43**, *Lachlan Macquarie*; *Ticket of Leave*; **p.44**, Augustus Earle, *View from the Summit of Mount York Looking Towards Bathurst Plains, Convicts Breaking Stones*; **p.45**, Augustus Earle, *First Sydney Lighthouse and Signal Station*; **p.47**, Antoine Cardon, *David Collins Esq*; **p.49**, Frank P Mahoney, *Convicts Plundering Homesteads*; **p.52**, Charles Hutchins, *North View of Eagle Hawk Neck which joins Tasman's Peninsula to the main land of Van Diemen's Land*; **p.54**, J.W. Beattie, *Port Arthur During Occupation*; **p.54**, Benjamin Duterrau, *Portrait of Governor Arthur*; **p.56**, *Convict Uprising at Castle Hill 1804*; **p.57**, Joseph Lycett, *Newcastle, New South Wales*; *Moreton Bay New South Wales*; **p.58**, Thomas Seller, *Settlement at Norfolk Island*; *Martin Cash*; **p.60**, Augustus Earle, *Female Penitentiary or Factory, Parramata* [sic]; **p.61**, John Skinner Prout, *The Female Factory from Proctor's Quarry*; **p.63**, Fremantle.

By permission of the National Library of Australia and *The Medical Journal of Australia*: p.44, Ford E. *The life and works of William Redfern*. MJA 1892 © Copyright 1892 *The Medical Journal of Australia*, reproduced with permission.

By permission of the Image Library, State Library of New South Wales: p.18, William Bradley, *Sirius and Convoy in Table Bay*; **p.21**, William Bradley, *Entrance of Port Jackson*; **p.26**, Reverend Richard Johnson.

By permission of the owners: p.42, *Portrait of John Macarthur,* private collection.

CONTENTS

INTRODUCTION

Captain Arthur Phillip,
the first governor of the
colony of New South Wales.

Modern Australia had its beginnings in January 1788, when the 11 sailing ships that made up what we now call the 'First Fleet' arrived in Port Jackson, which is now more commonly known as Sydney Harbour. It was the end of a voyage that had begun in Portsmouth, England, more than nine months earlier. On 26 January, the first people from these ships came ashore to form the new settlement that became known as Sydney Town. They landed on the shores of a bay that was named Sydney Cove, but which is now generally called Circular Quay. Of the 1500 or so people on board these ships, almost 800 were convicts—people from Britain and Ireland who had been convicted of crimes and who were being sent as punishment to New South Wales, about as far from their homes as it was possible to go. This punishment was called 'transportation'. About two out of every three of these convicts were male. Most of the others on board were members of the ships' crews, and soldiers—most of them marines and some of them officers—who were to guard and control the convicts. Commanding the First Fleet was Captain Arthur Phillip. Phillip was to be the first governor of the new colony. Others on board the First Fleet included a chaplain, a judge, a doctor and a surveyor, whose job it would be to make plans for building up the new settlement.

The 800 or so prisoners on the First Fleet were the first of about 160 000 convicted criminals who were sent from Britain to the Australian colonies over the next 80 years. Only about 20 000 of these convicts were women. About half of all the convicts came to New South Wales, which for most of the convict period included the present states of Victoria and Queensland. By 1849, when Victoria separated from New South Wales, transportation to eastern Australia had ceased. In any case, only a very small number of convicts were ever sent to the part of New South Wales that is now Victoria. Queensland became a separate colony in 1859, 20 years after the last convicts had been sent there. Like Sydney, Brisbane, the capital of Queensland, was originally founded as a convict settlement.

Almost 70 000 convicts were sent to Tasmania, which until 1825 was still part of New South Wales. During the period that convicts were being sent there, Tasmania was known as Van Diemen's Land. More than half the convicts who were sent to Van Diemen's Land arrived there during the 1840s and early 1850s. The first white people to come to Western Australia were free settlers and it was not until 1850 that convicts came to the west. In 1852, when transportation to Tasmania ceased, Western Australia was the only colony still receiving convicts. Transportation to the west ended in 1868, thus bringing to an end the 80 years of what is often called Australia's 'convict era'.

Who were the convicts?

About six out of every 10 convicts who came to Australia during the 80 years of the convict era were from England. Most of them were from the capital, London, or from other big English industrial cities such as Birmingham, Manchester and Sheffield. About three out of every 10 were from Ireland, which at that time was governed by Britain. Again, most of the Irish convicts were from the larger cities, such as Dublin and Belfast. Only very small numbers of convicts came from the other parts of Britain—Scotland and Wales.

About half of all the convicts were transported for a period of seven years. About one quarter were sentenced to 14 years transportation and the rest received life sentences. As you will read later, however, many convicts were released well before they had served their sentences. Many remained in the colonies to lead satisfying lives as free people; some became famous and made large fortunes.

For many, convict life was miserable and work was harsh. Those who defied the authorities or committed crimes while serving their sentences were severely punished. Life at so-called 'penal settlements', where serious offenders were sent, was often almost unbearable. Many other convicts, however, found life in the convict colonies much more pleasant than the life they had previously lived in England, in cities where poverty and squalor were the rule rather than the exception.

A lot of convicts were lucky to be sent to Australia. These included large numbers of people who had originally been sentenced to death in Britain, but whose sentences had been changed to transportation. At the end of the 18th century in Britain, people could be hanged for a wide range of crimes. Today, we would not consider some of these crimes, such as shoplifting or sheep or horse stealing, to be particularly serious. Most of the convicts in the First Fleet and in the early days of the colonies were guilty of theft or robbery, sometimes of fairly small amounts of money or goods. Later on in the 19th century, as British laws were changed, transportation was generally reserved for more serious offences such as crimes of violence, or large-scale robbery. By the 1830s, most of the people being sent to the colonies were people that we would think of as serious criminals.

BRITAIN IN THE LATE 1700S

In England and Ireland during the 18th century, some people, both in the country and in the towns, dressed in fine clothes, ate good food and lived in splendid houses. Most people, however, did not. Many, in fact, were extremely poor and lived in squalid conditions. One of the reasons for this widespread poverty was the spread of what we now call the Industrial Revolution.

The spread of factories

The age we live in today is often referred to as the 'information age' or the 'age of technology'. This is because the development of new technology, and especially computers, in the second half of the 1900s, brought about a huge change in the way people in our society can find information and communicate with each other. These changes have revolutionised the way many people live and work. For example, computers and even robots now do many of the jobs that only a few years ago people did by hand.

Something rather similar was happening in England in the 1700s. New machines were being invented that changed the way people worked and lived. As new machinery was invented, clothing, furniture and other goods that people had previously made in small workshops, or in their own homes, were manufactured more and more in large factories. Machines changed the nature of farming, too. They started to force people out of farm-working jobs and into the cities in search of factory work.

Increasing crime

As a result, the population of many British cities increased rapidly. Many people were unable to find work. Factory owners often preferred to employ children, some as young as eight or nine, because they could pay them almost nothing and make them work extremely hard. People who did have jobs often worked very long hours, in dirty, dangerous and unhealthy conditions, for very little money. Even working people often could not afford to eat properly or to live in decent houses. Filthy, disease-ridden and terribly overcrowded slum areas grew up in parts of London and other cities. Largely as a result of these living conditions, more and more people became thieves or even robbers. Some even went out into the countryside and held up and robbed rich people travelling in coaches. These criminals were known as highwaymen. The killing or stealing of horses, sheep and other farm animals became a very common crime in country areas. In the cities many children became practised criminals, picking the pockets of people in the streets, especially in crowded places. Adult criminals often employed children to steal for them.

The authorities reacted to the ever-growing crime rate by making penalties harsher. By the 1770s in Britain, there were more than 150 offences that carried the death penalty. People were executed by being hanged in public. Hangings often attracted huge crowds of curious and excited spectators. Public hangings were supposed to set a stern example to those who witnessed them, but these events often seemed more like public festivities.

A public hanging in London in the 18th century.

A prison hulk in Portsmouth Harbour, England, in the 1770s.

Spectators bought refreshments from food and drink sellers and were entertained by strolling musicians and actors. Pickpockets often did very well on these occasions, snatching money and other items from unwary spectators and then disappearing quickly into the crowd.

Transportation

As crime increased, English prisons became hopelessly overcrowded. In Australia today prisons are often dangerous and unpleasant, but in English prisons of the 18th century conditions were atrocious. Large numbers of prisoners, sometimes with their hands and feet chained, were often herded into small, bare cells. The toilet for a cell might be no more than an open trench. Rats and lice often infested these prisons, bringing with them typhoid fever, which was known as 'gaol fever' and which killed many prisoners. The food was very poor, and prisoners sometimes died of starvation. Not surprisingly, fights, which often ended in serious injury or death, were common.

British prisons became even more over-crowded after 1775. In that year the American War of Independence broke out. British colonies in what is now the eastern United States of America rebelled against British rule and went to war to gain their independence. For almost 60 years, Britain had been sending convicted criminals to some of its American colonies, where they worked alongside slaves on cotton plantations. As long as the War of Independence lasted these prisoners had to be kept at home. Rotten old ships, called prison hulks, were moored in British harbours and rivers to house the prisoners that would not fit in the gaols. As soon as Britain won the war against the American rebels, it was believed, these prisoners could be shipped off once again to Britain's American colonies. But the American rebels won the war and the United States of America was born—and Britain was left with nowhere to send its unwanted criminals.

FROM ENDEAVOUR TO FIRST FLEET

As you read on page 6, the first European settlers arrived in New South Wales in January 1788, but the story of white settlement in Australia began almost 20 years before that. In August 1768, a small three-masted sailing ship, the *Endeavour*, left Plymouth, on the south coast of England, bound for the distant waters of the Pacific Ocean. On board the *Endeavour* were 94 men, under the command of Captain James Cook. The *Endeavour* was setting out on an expedition of both science and discovery. The first part of the voyage was to take the *Endeavour* to the island of Tahiti, which was thought to be the best place to observe an event known as the 'transit of Venus'. The transit of Venus occurs once every 105 years, when the planet Venus comes between the Earth and the Sun. A number of scientists, including the astronomer Charles Green, were among the people on board. Also on board was a 27-year-old botanist, Joseph Banks. Banks, who was a rich man, actually asked permission to go on this expedition, and took with him another botanist, four artists and a large amount of scientific equipment. The expedition probably cost Banks about 10 000 pounds, a huge amount of money in those days.

Once this part of the mission was completed, Cook had orders from the British government to sail further south into what was then unknown territory. Many people in Britain and in Europe at that time believed that there was a huge continent covering most of the southern part of the Earth. The British government hoped that Cook would discover this and claim it as a British possession. In July 1769, the *Endeavour*

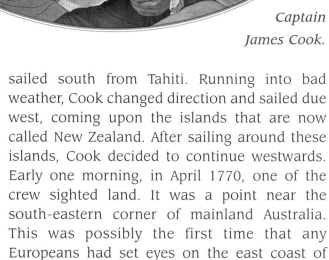

Captain James Cook.

sailed south from Tahiti. Running into bad weather, Cook changed direction and sailed due west, coming upon the islands that are now called New Zealand. After sailing around these islands, Cook decided to continue westwards. Early one morning, in April 1770, one of the crew sighted land. It was a point near the south-eastern corner of mainland Australia. This was possibly the first time that any Europeans had set eyes on the east coast of mainland Australia.

Over the next four months, Cook sailed the *Endeavour* along the entire length of Australia's eastern coast, naming many places along the way, and coming ashore a number of times. The first place that Cook landed was located in a wide bay a little south of where Sydney now stands. Here Banks and the other botanists collected many interesting plant species that were completely new to them. Because of these plant discoveries, they named the bay Botany Bay. It is still called that today.

*Cook's landing at
Botany Bay in 1770.*

Banks' recommendation

At first, it seems, Cook and Banks had very different impressions of the eastern part of Australia, which Cook named New South Wales. In his journal, Cook wrote:

'This Eastern side is not [a] barren and Miserable Country. . . In this Extensive Country it can never be doubted but what most sorts of Grain, Fruits, Roots etc would flourish here were they once brought hither, planted and cultivated . . . and here are Provender [fodder] for more Cattle at all seasons of the year than can ever be brought into this Country.'

In his journal, however, Banks described the country he saw as 'uncommon barren' and not suitable for crops or cattle.

As a result of his journey in the *Endeavour*, and the scientific observations he made, Banks became a famous and influential public figure in England. People at the highest levels of government often came to him for advice. By 1779, eight years after the *Endeavour* had returned to England, Banks must have changed his mind about New South Wales. As you read on page 9, by this time prisons in England were overflowing and ridden with disease. Britain could no longer transport its prisoners to North America and the government badly wanted to find a new place to send them. Banks offered a solution: establish a penal colony at Botany Bay in New South Wales. He told a special committee that had been set up to deal with the problem that the land around Botany Bay was fertile and that, within a year of arriving, people in the new settlement would be able to produce enough food for their needs.

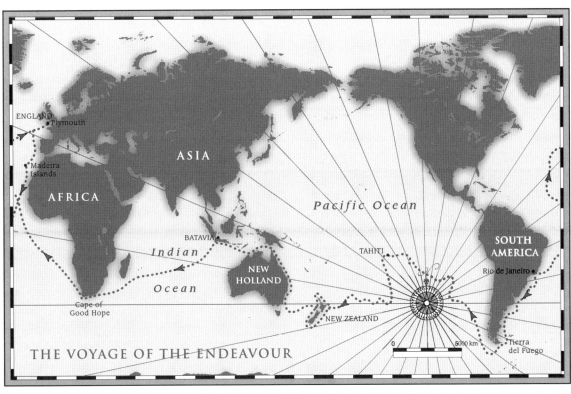

THE VOYAGE OF THE ENDEAVOUR

He even suggested that as the colony grew larger, it would need to import manufactured products from England. This would be good for English industry.

As far as we know, Banks was the first to suggest this solution. Because of this, he is often referred to as 'the father of modern Australia'.

Sir Joseph Banks.

Making a decision

There were a number of places that the British government could have used to get rid of its unwanted criminals. It had colonies in Canada in North America, in Gambia in west Africa, in southern Africa and in the West Indies in the Caribbean Sea. None of these places proved to be suitable. Canada was already being settled by free people from Britain and France. They certainly did not want criminals sent there. The climate in southern Africa was very hot and the land sandy and barren. Black slaves were already working in the sugar plantations in the West Indies and slave owners did not want white convicts working there. In any case, tropical diseases would no doubt have killed convicts who were not used to the hot, humid conditions. Gambia, which was also in the tropics, had proved this point. In 1775, 700 convicts had been sent to Gambia. Most of them had died of tropical diseases or of hunger.

In 1779, Britain was still engaged in the American War of Independence, and nothing was done about Banks' suggestion. At this stage, the British government was still confident that it would defeat the American revolutionaries and continue to send convicts to its American colonies. In 1881, the American revolutionaries finally defeated the British. No more convicts could be sent to North America.

Matra, Young and Sydney

In 1783, William Matra, who had been a sailor on Cook's *Endeavour* voyage, suggested setting up a colony in New South Wales. Originally, Matra thought that only free people should settle this colony. The following year he changed his mind, now suggesting that the government should send both free settlers and convicts. Soon after, Sir George Young, an admiral in the British navy, took up the same theme. He stressed the advantages that a colony on the shores of the Pacific would have for British trade and defence. He also pointed out that the cost of sending 'felons' to the other end of the world would be little more than the cost of keeping them in prisons in England. Lord Sydney, who was the Home Secretary in the British government, also found the idea attractive. As Home Secretary, Sydney was the British minister responsible for matters concerned with the colonies. In April 1785, a committee was set up to try and resolve the matter, but the members were unable to make up their minds and no firm recommendations were made.

Meanwhile, the crime rate was rising and prisoners were escaping quite easily from the hulks. Newspapers were reporting the breakdown of law and order, often giving highly exaggerated reports of the exploits of villainous criminal gangs. A member of the British parliament, Edmund Burke, was also guilty of gross exaggeration when he announced that there were 100 000 people in English gaols. In fact, there were fewer than 7500 prisoners, and only about 4000 of these had been convicted of crimes for which they could be transported.

In March 1786, an event occurred which frightened many people and confirmed their worst fears. Prisoners on a hulk in Plymouth Harbour staged a violent riot. By the time this riot was over, eight prisoners had been shot dead by their guards and almost 40 were wounded.

Not long after this, in August 1786, the government finally decided to set up a penal colony. As Lord Sydney said, when he announced the decision to the British parliament: 'His Majesty has thought it advisable to fix upon Botany Bay, situated on the coast of New South Wales'. In another speech to the parliament, the king, George III, gave only one reason for the decision: 'in order to remove the inconvenience which arose from the crowded state of the gaols'.

However, Botany Bay had more to offer than just a way of getting rid of unwanted criminals. French explorers were active in the South Pacific. Setting up a colony in New South Wales would prevent the French from getting there first. Relations between Britain and France were not good at the time, especially as French soldiers had helped American revolutionaries defeat the British in the American War of Independence. If British and French warships ever clashed in the Pacific, Botany Bay would provide a valuable British base.

Norfolk Island was another reason. Norfolk Island is a small island, about 40 square kilometres in area, situated in the Pacific, about 1500 kilometres north-east of Sydney. Cook had discovered the island, which was uninhabited, in 1774, this time as captain of the *Resolution*. Here he found large numbers of sturdy pine trees that would make excellent masts for ships. Flax also grew there, and this, he thought, would be ideal for making sails and ropes for British ships.

Arthur Phillip

The man chosen to lead the expedition to New South Wales and to become the first governor of the new colony was Arthur Phillip. Phillip was a former naval commander with an impressive war record. In 1786, Phillip was 48 years

The Endeavour.

old. He had retired from the navy two years earlier and was living on a farm in the south of England. When Lord Sydney suggested to Phillip that he take on the job, Phillip accepted. Perhaps the quiet life of a solitary farmer did not suit this man of action. At this stage Phillip had few family ties in England. His first marriage had broken up several years before.

Phillip needed to employ all his ability as an organiser to get things ready for the voyage. The British government made available 11 ships for the voyage to New South Wales, but it left many details of the voyage unplanned. Government officials had not allowed enough food for the voyage or enough equipment for growing crops once the ships reached New South Wales. There was no provision made for clothes for the female convicts, for ammunition for the soldiers' guns or for medical supplies. And no-one had thought of providing rum for the soldiers and wine for the officers and officials. As well, the British government had planned to send only 10 ships. Phillip soon realised that was not enough, and insisted that another ship was necessary.

Phillip ensured that by the time the 11 ships of the First Fleet sailed out of Portsmouth Harbour, they were properly equipped for the voyage and for the founding of a settlement. If he hadn't, the voyage would probably have been a disaster.

A SUCCESSFUL VOYAGE

At four o'clock on the morning of 13 May 1787, a fleet of 12 ships sailed out of Portsmouth Harbour on the southern coast of England. These were the 11 ships of the First Fleet and an extra ship, HMS *Hyaena*, which was to accompany the fleet for its first week at sea. Almost no-one in England noticed or knew about the departure of this fleet. Few people in those days read newspapers, and even if they did, they could easily have missed the references to the fleet that was about to sail to the other side of the world. Many people in Portsmouth would have been aware that a fleet had been assembled over the previous few months and would have seen convicts being rowed out to the ships. The day before the departure, troops lined the streets as large numbers of wagons lumbered through the town carrying the last convicts to be taken on board.

The First Fleet started its voyage seven months late. Originally, the ships were supposed to set sail in October 1786. If they had left then, the voyage would almost certainly have been a disaster, because, as you read on page 13, proper preparations had not been made. Phillip was determined that the ships would not leave until he was satisfied that they were properly fitted out and had enough provisions.

By the time they left, many of those on board must have experienced a feeling of relief. Some had already been waiting on board for months, confined mainly below decks and kept in chains. Sixteen convicts had died during the cold winter months and others had become ill. Many convicts had only recently been transferred from the filthy and overcrowded convict hulks on the River Thames near London; others had been waiting in similar conditions in prisons on land. One officer later wrote that as the last convicts were being rowed out to the ships, they gave a rousing three cheers. What lay ahead of them was unknown, but it could hardly be worse than what they had already endured since they were sentenced. Some were no doubt thankful to still be alive—many of these convicts had been sentenced to death, but were reprieved and sent instead to New South Wales. Two male convicts, though, had reason to be thankful for all the delays. They received pardons, and were set free, just days before the fleet set sail.

Convicts being rowed out to the ships that would transport them to New South Wales.

Good fortune

The convicts, marines, crewmen, officers and officials on the First Fleet were probably fortunate that Phillip was in charge of the fleet and that the British government was in charge of organising the voyage. Most of the voyages that had transported convicts to the American colonies had been organised by private shipowners, who provided and fitted out the transport ships and shipped the convicts for a fee. Not surprisingly, these shipowners were generally much more interested in cutting costs than in looking after the welfare of their convict cargoes. As a result, conditions on board were often dreadful and many convicts did not survive these journeys.

Conditions on the First Fleet were certainly crowded and uncomfortable, especially for the convicts, but at least the ships had been adequately provisioned—in spite of the original problems—and Phillip was a skilled and conscientious commander. Only 48 people died during the long voyage, which lasted more than eight months. That seems a lot to us today, but for those times it was an extremely good result. Some of these people died as a result of accidents at sea and many who died of illness were seriously ill before they set sail.

The ships

A number of the ferries that now take passengers from Circular Quay to various destinations around Sydney Harbour are named after some of the ships of the First Fleet. Even though these ferries are smaller than the largest ferries that sail around the harbour, they are at least as large as some of the ships that they are named after. While the present-day ferries travel short distances on Sydney Harbour, the First Fleet ships sailed more than 20 000 kilometres through some of the world's roughest seas.

The 750 or so First Fleet convicts sailed on only six of the 11 ships. These were known as the transport ships, or transports. The largest of these was the *Alexander*, which measured 35 metres long and 9 metres wide and weighed 461 tonnes. The smallest was the *Friendship*, which weighed 279 tonnes. In between were the *Scarborough*, which, at 439 tonnes, was almost as large as the *Alexander*; the *Charlotte*, the *Lady Penrhyn* and the *Prince of Wales*. Between them, the two largest transports, the *Alexander* and the *Scarborough*, carried just over 400 male convicts. The *Lady Penrhyn* carried just over 100 convicts, all of whom were female, while the *Prince of Wales* had about 50 convicts, only one of whom was male. The other transports carried a mixture of male and female convicts.

Three more ships, known as storeships, carried the food and other equipment needed for creating a new settlement. These were the *Fishburn*, the *Golden Grove* and the *Borrowdale*. The remaining two ships were known as escort ships. They did not carry any convicts or stores, but were armed with cannons in case the fleet was attacked at sea. The largest of the two escort ships, and the largest member of the First Fleet, was HMS *Sirius*, which weighed 551 tonnes and was 34 metres long and 10 metres wide. The *Sirius* was the leader, or flagship, of the fleet. It carried 160 people, including the most senior military and naval officers. Phillip was on board the *Sirius* and so too were two officers who would later become governors of the colony of New South Wales—Captain John Hunter and Lieutenant Philip Gidley King.

The other escort ship, HMS *Supply*, was the smallest member of the fleet. The *Supply* weighed only 173 tonnes, was a mere 21 metres long and 8 metres wide. The *Sirius* and *Supply* were the only two ships that belonged to the British Navy. The other nine were hired from private shipowners.

The voyage

On 18 January 1788, 250 days after setting out, the *Supply* sailed into Botany Bay, one day ahead of the *Alexander*, the *Scarborough* and the *Friendship*, and two days ahead of the rest of the fleet. About three-quarters of the time taken to reach Botany Bay had been spent at sea; a total of 68 days had been spent in three ports at which the fleet had stopped.

The first leg of the voyage lasted three weeks and took the ships to the port of Santa Cruz on the island of Tenerife in the Canary Islands, off the north-west coast of Africa. It

View of the island of Tenerife.

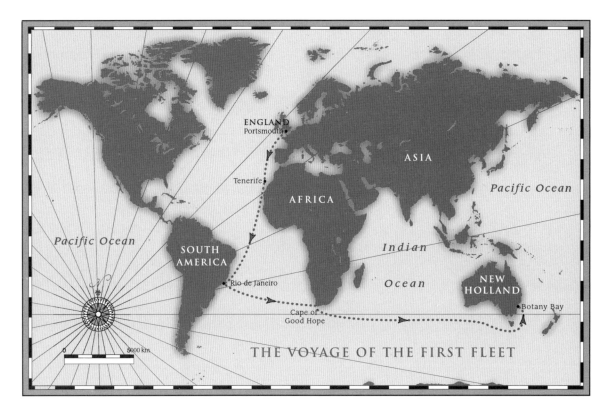

ENGLAND
Portsmouth

Tenerife

ASIA

Pacific Ocean

AFRICA

Pacific Ocean

SOUTH
AMERICA

Rio de Janeiro

Indian

Ocean

NEW
HOLLAND

Botany Bay

Cape of
Good Hope

0   5000 km.

THE VOYAGE OF THE FIRST FLEET

was a turbulent start. For most of the time the waters of the North Atlantic Ocean were rough. When, on 20 May, the *Hyaena* turned around to return to England, the weather was so bad that most of the letters that convicts and crewmen had already written to people back in England could not be collected from the various ships.

There were other troubles as well. On 18 May, just five days after setting out, two convicts on the *Scarborough* attempted a mutiny. They encouraged other convicts to take over the ship and sail it away from the rest of the fleet, and managed to gather tools and weapons for the uprising. The attempt failed because a convict informed officers of the plot. The ringleaders, Phillip Farrell and Thomas Griffiths, were transferred to the *Sirius*, where they were each given a flogging of 24 lashes, and placed in irons. This was the first of many such punishments during the voyage.

Only three days earlier, on 15 May, Phillip had given orders that the chains be removed from the convicts' arms and legs. Many of the officers disagreed with this order, but Phillip realised that prisoners in irons could not clothe and wash themselves properly and were much more likely to become ill. In any case, in the rough weather many convicts, confined for

much of the time below decks in almost airless compartments (there were no windows or portholes in the convicts' quarters), became violently seasick. So too did many of the officers. By the time the First Fleet reached Tenerife, eight convicts and one seaman (William Mead, of the *Scarborough*) had died.

The Canary Islands were then one of Spain's colonies. The Spanish governor gave Captain Phillip permission to collect fresh supplies of water and food, and for the next seven days small boats plied between the shore and the ships of the fleet, carrying casks of water and loads of fresh meat and vegetables. While many of the officers took the opportunity to go ashore, the convicts were kept on board their ships. They were put to work in the day cleaning the decks and were given opportunities to take fresh air and exercise. However, the intense tropical heat made conditions extremely uncomfortable and frequent downpours of rain meant that they spent long periods sweating in the stuffy conditions below deck.

John Power, one of the most desperate convicts on the *Alexander*, almost escaped at Santa Cruz. One night during the stay there, he managed to climb unobserved down the anchor rope and into a dinghy. He rowed to a Dutch ship that was anchored nearby, where he tried to convince the crew to take him on board as a seaman. The Dutch refused, and Power made it to shore. Unfortunately for him, the dinghy was spotted next morning by a search party and he was recaptured. Back on board, he was placed in irons. Power would be in trouble again soon afterwards.

To Rio de Janeiro

The next port of call was the Brazilian port of Rio de Janeiro, on the eastern coast of South America. This was a long haul of eight weeks at sea. Originally Phillip had intended to call at the Cape Verde Islands, off the extreme western coast of North Africa. He wished to replenish the supplies of water and fresh fruit and vegetables that had been collected at Tenerife. Phillip well understood that these foods offered protection against scurvy, a disease that many people at sea suffered and died from in those days. However, nine days after leaving Tenerife, as the ships approached the entrance to Port Praya on the island of St Triago, Phillip decided that the conditions were too dangerous and he ordered the fleet to continue without stopping.

As the fleet sailed to the south-west, weather conditions improved, but by early July, when they were still only about halfway to Rio, water supplies were running low and had to be rationed. After weeks at sea in these trying circumstances, discipline among the convicts and some marines and crewmen began to break down. Floggings were used to restore order and to serve as an example to others. On 25 June, a marine on the *Prince of Wales*, Robert Ryan, was sentenced to 300 lashes for disobeying orders. He collapsed after receiving 175 lashes and the rest of the punishment was given later. In general during the voyage, marines were punished much more severely than convict offenders.

The guards and officers found many of the women convicts particularly hard to control. Many of them were given rum by the marines and were frequently drunk. They also often found their way into the marines' and seamen's quarters at night, and frequently got into fights.

William Bradley, an officer on one of the ships, painted this picture of Rio de Janeiro.

Elizabeth Dudgeon was one of a group on the *Friendship* known as the 'fighting five'. She had been put in irons at Tenerife for fighting and once at sea was soon in trouble again. One day, she lost her temper and savagely swore at one of the ship's officers. The officer took matters into his own hands, and ordered her to be flogged with a piece of rope. Unlike male convicts and seamen and marines, female convicts were rarely flogged.

Towards the end of July, about two weeks before the fleet reached Rio de Janeiro, rough weather caused the deaths of two convicts. A male convict on the *Alexander* was blown overboard and drowned in a storm that damaged the masts and sails of several ships. Jane Bonner, on the *Prince of Wales*, died after being hit on the head by a wildly swinging lifeboat.

When, on Sunday 5 August 1787, the fleet sailed into the beautiful harbour at Rio, it received a warm welcome. Brazil was a colony of Portugal, and Phillip, who had once served in the Portuguese navy, could speak Portuguese. The governor treated Phillip and his officers as special guests. It took a month to provision the ships for the next part of the voyage and the fleet's officers were able to spend much of this time on shore. The convicts were less fortunate. They remained on their ships, much of the time confined below decks.

To the Cape of Good Hope

On 4 September 1787, the fleet sailed out of the harbour at Rio, bound for Cape Town, on the southern tip of the African continent. This was to be its last port of call before it began the last, longest and most difficult leg of the voyage.

By most accounts this part of the voyage went relatively smoothly. Phillip wrote that this passage was 'not marked by any extraordinary incidents', and Watkin Tench, a captain of marines on the *Charlotte*, wrote in his diary that 'nothing worth relating happened'.

There were, however, a number of serious incidents that marred this journey. There were several periods of violent storms and

William Bradley painted this picture of the fleet anchored at Cape Town.

rough seas. On 19 September, just two weeks after the fleet left Rio, William Brown, who was described as a 'very well-behaved convict', fell overboard from the *Charlotte* while bringing in some clothing that he had hung out to dry. His body was not recovered. Ten days later, Thomas Mason, the nine-month-old son of Betty Mason, a convict on the *Friendship*, died at two o'clock in the morning. The baby boy, who had been sick during the whole of the voyage, was born in London's Newgate Prison, where his mother was awaiting transportation. He and his unfortunate mother had been on board the *Friendship* for almost a month before the fleet sailed from Portsmouth.

On 6 October the fleet was sailing through thick fog and heavy rain. In these conditions people on one ship could not see other ships of the fleet. John Power, who had tried to escape in Rio, decided to take advantage of the situation. He and several other convicts on the *Alexander* had managed to arm themselves with knives and pistols and attempted to take over the ship. The attempt, which had clearly been carefully planned, may well have succeeded if one of the convicts had not lost his nerve and reported the uprising to the ship's captain. Alerted to the danger, the marines overcame the convicts and arrested the ringleaders. Power and his accomplices were taken on board the *Sirius*, where Phillip had them flogged and placed in irons for the rest of the voyage. The convict who had informed on them was transferred to the *Scarborough* for his own safety. A week after this disturbing incident, the fleet arrived safely in Table Bay at the Cape of Good Hope.

Van Graaf, the Dutch governor of the Cape Province, was much less welcoming to Phillip and his fleet than the Portuguese governor of Rio had been. At first, he refused to supply provisions, saying that the colony was short of food. For more than a week, he would supply them with nothing but bread. The tension and the inactivity led to outbreaks of fighting among the convicts and drunkenness among the seamen and marines.

Eventually, Phillip was able to persuade the Dutch to sell their visitors the meat and vegetables they needed immediately and the livestock, poultry, seeds and plants they would require to found a settlement in the unknown land that they were headed for.

For the convicts, the stay in Table Bay must have been particularly distressing. From the decks of their ships, they could see the grizzly sight of dead criminals hanging from gallows on the shore and large wheels on which others had been tortured to death. Such cruel sights must have led some to wonder whether similar punishments would await those who committed serious offences in their new, but unchosen, land. Some, such as 17-year-old Thomas Barrett, may well have had an inkling that their lives would soon end in a similar fashion. Barrett was to be the first person hanged in New South Wales. You can read more about him on page 26.

Across the southern oceans

The last leg of the voyage was the longest and most difficult. The ships sailed out of Cape Town on 12 November 1787 and arrived at Botany Bay almost 10 weeks later, between 18 and 20 January 1788. For this part of the voyage, Phillip sailed on the *Supply*. His plan was to split the fleet into two parts. The *Supply* and the other three fastest sailing ships would go on ahead and arrive at Botany Bay earlier than the rest. This would allow him to set up camp and make plans for the settlement before the remaining ships arrived.

However, violent storms lashed the fleet during much of the trip, and the *Supply* was not able to keep up its usual speed. As well, winds blowing from the east, instead of from the west, held up the fleet during the first and last weeks. As a result, many of the animals that had been taken on board at the Cape died when their fodder ran out.

The convicts suffered worst of all from the violent weather as huge waves broke over the transports and soaked them and their cramped quarters. In spite of the weather, the ships survived this last part of the voyage with little damage. Surprisingly, too, only one person died by accident. On the night of 23 November, a seaman on the *Prince of Wales* was blown overboard while climbing a mast. The next day on the same ship a convict, Elenor McCave, gave birth to a dead child. There was an outbreak of dysentery on the *Charlotte*, and several convicts died from the disease, one of them on Christmas Day. The last convict death during the voyage occurred on 9 January. On that morning John Thomson died. The ship's surgeon, John White, wrote that the unfortunate convict was 'worn out with melancholy and long confinement'. 'Had he lived,' continued White, 'I think he would have proved a very deserving member of society.'

The *Supply*, with Phillip on board, reached Botany Bay on 18 January. The rest of the fleet came in over the next two days.

A change of plan

Phillip was not impressed with Botany Bay. The water was shallow and the bay did not seem to offer protection from storms. Worse still, the soil seemed sandy and infertile. It was

Phillip sailing into Port Jackson for the first time.

William Bradley's painting of the First Fleet sailing into Port Jackson on 26 January 1788.

not the place that the reports by James Cook and Joseph Banks had led him to expect. So, instead of landing the convicts and supplies, Phillip took three small boats and sailed further north. Just a few kilometres up the coast, he sailed into Port Jackson. There he discovered what he described as 'the finest harbour in the world, in which a thousand sail of the line may ride in the most perfect security'. In an inlet of this harbour, Phillip decided to found the new colony. Phillip named this inlet Sydney Cove, after Lord Sydney, the Home Secretary in the British Government (you read about Lord Sydney on page 12).

Phillip sailed back to Botany Bay and ordered the other ships to sail to Port Jackson. On 26 January 1788, Phillip and a small group of marines and convicts went ashore and raised the British flag. It was another 11 days before all the convicts and stores from the ships had been brought ashore. The last convicts to be disembarked were the women, who came ashore on 6 February.

Soon afterwards, nine of the 11 ships of the First Fleet sailed away, leaving behind only the *Sirius* and the *Supply*. These two ships were now the new colony's only link with the outside world.

SOME FIRST FLEETERS

We know very little about many of the convicts who came to New South Wales on the First Fleet. As you read in the previous section, a number of convicts, such as John Power, drew attention to themselves by the way they behaved on the voyage. Others were noticed because they suffered accidents or died as the result of sickness. Most of what we know was recorded by about 11 officers who kept diaries of the voyage and of the early days of the new settlement. Some of these officers and other marines also wrote letters that have survived and that throw some light on the lives and the fate of some of the convicts. The experiences of most convicts on the First Fleet, however, remain a mystery to us. The diary writers in general had little interest in individual convicts and some of them expressed contempt for them. The surgeon on board the *Lady Penrhyn*, Arthur Bowes Smith, described the women convicts on his ship as the most 'abandon'd set of wretches collected in one place at any period' and added that the same applied 'with respect to all Convicts in the fleet'.

From the evidence we have, it seems that most of the First Fleet convicts were practised criminals. Among them were cattle, horse and sheep stealers, forgers of coins and bank notes, highway robbers and receivers of stolen goods. A few had committed robbery with violence. The great majority, however, were convicted of petty theft. They were to serve seven years in New South Wales because they had stolen small amounts of money, or items of food, clothing or jewellery. In many cases, these people were driven to commit these crimes by poverty or hunger and stole in order to survive.

Oldest and youngest

Most of the convicts on the First Fleet were quite young people, and most of them came from London. The average age seems to have been about 27. The British government realised that the new colony would have a better chance of succeeding with a population of younger people.

There were some older people. The oldest convict was a woman, Dorothy Handlyn, who sailed on the *Lady Penrhyn*. She was 82, and was sentenced to seven years transportation for giving false evidence in court. This poor woman was to serve less than two of those years. In 1789, she hanged herself from a tree in Sydney Cove and so became the first person that we know of who committed suicide in the colony. The oldest man was Joseph Owen. He was in his sixties and sailed on the *Friendship*.

One convict who was probably forced into a life of crime was the youngest of the First Fleet convicts. John Hudson was only 13 when the fleet set sail. He was only nine when, in 1783, he was sentenced to seven years transportation. As

Boy convicts at Woolwich, near London, being taken on board a transport ship bound for New South Wales.

Britain had nowhere to send convicts in 1783, young Hudson spent several months in Newgate Prison, before being transferred to one of the terrible prison hulks, where he remained for the next three years.

At the age of nine, Hudson had long been an orphan. At his trial in London's Old Bailey court he stated that he was 'sometimes a chimney sweeper'. Many poor young boys at the time were employed as chimneysweeps. Climbing up and cleaning out filthy chimneys was a dangerous and unhealthy occupation. The boys, who often came from orphanages, were usually controlled by a 'master sweeper', who often paid them little or nothing for their work, thus forcing the boys to beg or steal food and clothing.

In October 1783 Hudson and another boy broke into a London house and stole some clothes. The owner of the house found soot on some of his furniture and immediately suspected that a chimneysweep was one of the thieves. A few days later, Hudson was seen picking up the stolen goods from a hiding place, and was arrested. At his trial, Hudson was lucky not to be sentenced to death. Boys as young as nine could be hanged in Britain in those days. The judge seemed to take pity on the young law-breaker. He found the boy guilty of breaking and entering, but not of burglary.

We do not know very much about John Hudson's life after he arrived in New South Wales on board the *Friendship*. We know from some records that in March 1790 he was sent to Norfolk Island, where Phillip decided to set up a separate convict settlement in February 1788. The *Sirius* was the ship that took Hudson from Sydney. It was wrecked on a reef just before it arrived at Norfolk Island, but Hudson and everyone else on board managed to get ashore. We know that Hudson was still on the island almost a year later because records show that he was given 50 lashes for being out of bounds after dark. That is the last we know of the youngest convict to arrive on the First Fleet.

The youngest female convict was only a few months older than John Hudson. Elizabeth

Two young chimneysweeps in London.

Hayward was also a 13-year-old when she sailed on the *Lady Penrhyn*. When the First Fleet sailed, Elizabeth had already spent four months on board. Just before Christmas 1786, Elizabeth, who was apprenticed to a shoe-maker, stole some clothes from her employer and then made the mistake of trying to sell them. That is when she was caught. Her trial came up about a month later and she was sentenced to be transported to New South Wales for seven years.

When she arrived in the new colony, Elizabeth became a servant in the household of the Reverend Richard Johnson, the new colony's first chaplain. She may have been a troublesome servant, because in February 1789 she was sentenced to a whipping for being uncooperative. In March 1790 she, like John Hudson, sailed to Norfolk Island on the ill-fated

The **Sirius** *lies wrecked off Norfolk Island in 1790.*

Sirius's last voyage. She stayed on the island for 23 years, most of that time as a free woman, married to a Joseph Lowe. She died in Launceston, Tasmania, in 1836.

Children of convicts

John Hudson and Elizabeth Hayward were not the only children to sail with the First Fleet, and they were far from the youngest. Thirteen children of convicts, some of them just babies, set sail for New South Wales with their convict mothers. Three of these children died during the voyage. One was Thomas Mason, whom you read about on page 19. He was only about six months old when the fleet set sail. The two other children who died during the voyage were girls. One was Mary Lawson, the infant daughter of a convict, Isabella Lawson. Mary was born on the *Lady Penrhyn* less than three weeks after it left and died just over a week later. The other, Jane Davis, was not a convict's child. She was the daughter of John Davis, a marine, and his wife Martha. Jane was born on the *Prince of Wales* on 9 May 1787, just four days before it sailed. She died in July, before the ship reached Rio de Janeiro.

A total of 20 children were born during the voyage of the First Fleet, 10 of them to convict mothers. The fathers of some of these children were seamen or marines who had been aboard the convict ships some months before they set sail.

The Kables

Henry Kable was a child of three or four when he sailed with his convict parents, Henry Kable and Susannah Holmes, on the *Friendship*. Both parents had been convicted of housebreaking and sent to New South Wales for 14 years. Young Henry was born in Norwich prison and spent some months with his parents on a prison hulk before the fleet sailed.

On 10 February 1788, just two weeks after the fleet had arrived in Sydney, the Reverend Richard Johnson married five couples. These were the first marriages in the colony. One of the couples was Henry Kable and Susannah Holmes. The Kables went on to have another 10 children.

Henry Kable senior became one of the great success stories among the convicts. He obviously impressed Governor Phillip and was soon appointed to positions of responsibility. He was given the job of supervising other convicts and then became chief constable. He suffered a setback when he was dismissed from this position for selling rum to convicts. By the early 1800s Kable was both free and very wealthy. With two other ex-convicts, he set up a whaling and sealing business. By 1810 they were supplying sealskins and other products to the colony and exporting to places as far afield as Britain, China and India. In 1811, Kable left Sydney to live in Windsor, where he died in 1846 at the age of 84. Henry Kable junior shared his father's talent for business. As a young man he was a ship's officer and later went on to be a wealthy shipowner.

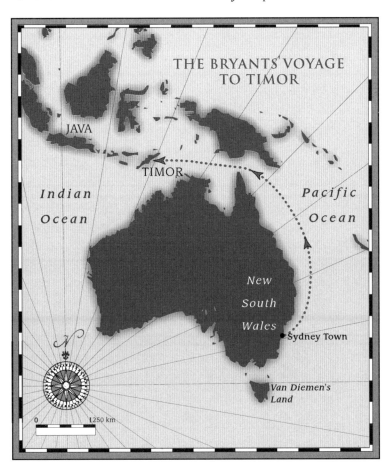

THE BRYANTS' VOYAGE TO TIMOR

JAVA

TIMOR

Indian Ocean

Pacific Ocean

New South Wales

Sydney Town

Van Diemen's Land

0   1250 km

Escape to Timor

Another of the couples that the Reverend Richard Johnson married on 10 February 1788 were the convicts Mary Brand and William Bryant. Both had come out on the *Charlotte*. During the voyage, Mary had given birth to a daughter. She named her Charlotte, after the ship. Both Mary and William were known on the *Charlotte* as very well-behaved convicts. Mary had been transported for stealing clothes; William, who was a fisherman from Cornwall, was sentenced for smuggling.

In the early days of the new colony, food soon became scarce. Bryant, whom Governor Phillip trusted, was put in charge of a fishing boat. However, when he was caught selling some of his catch, he was sentenced to a severe whipping. Mary and William decided to escape. With seven other convict men, they made their plans. In March 1791, both the *Supply* and the *Sirius*—the only First Fleet ships that still remained in the colony—sailed for Norfolk Island. The escapees seized their chance. Under cover of darkness, they scrambled into one of the governor's open boats and silently rowed out of the harbour. Along with Mary, William and the seven other convicts, were Mary's young daughter Charlotte and the Bryants' baby son, Emanuel.

The Bryants had decided to head for the Dutch-controlled island of Timor, near Java to the north-west of the Australian continent. Bryant had obtained a compass, some maps and other equipment from a visiting Dutch seaman. Against all the odds, the escapees sailed safely up the east coast of New South Wales, as all of eastern Australia was then known, around Cape York and across the north of the continent. Just over two months after leaving, they arrived safely in Timor. Strangely enough, this is where their most serious troubles began.

At first the Dutch governor of Timor welcomed them, thinking they were survivors of a shipwreck. Later, however, when he found out the truth, he arrested them and later handed them over to a visiting English captain who took them to Batavia, the Dutch capital of Java. Here, in December 1791, both William Bryant and the baby Emanuel died of a tropical fever. The surviving escapees were then sent to the Cape of Good Hope to await the *Gorgon*, a ship that was sailing from Sydney to England, taking back some marines who had finished their term of duty in the colony. On the way to the Cape, three of the seven male convicts died.

On board the *Gorgon*, Mary and the four convicts were treated with sympathy by the marines and their officers, who admired them for their heroic attempt at escaping. But tragedy struck in May 1792, when Charlotte, who was now three, died during the voyage. On arriving back in England, Mary and the four other covicts were taken straight to prison to await further punishment. However, the English newspapers got hold of the remarkable story of this 'girl from Botany Bay' and a number of prominent citizens pleaded with the government to pardon her. The pleas were accepted and Mary and the four male convicts were all freed.

Thomas Barrett

Seventeen days after the Reverend Richard Johnson performed the first marriages in the colony, he took part in a much more grisly public ceremony. On 27 February, at about 6.30 in the evening, he said prayers with a 17-year-old convict, Thomas Barrett, who soon after became the first person to be hanged in New South Wales. Barrett's offence was

The Reverend Richard Johnson.

stealing 'butter, pease and pork'. Just a month after the settlement had been established, it had become clear that providing enough food would be a difficult task and that the stealing of food could become a major problem in the colony. Phillip was determined to stamp it out and so made an example of the unfortunate Barrett. Two other convicts who were sentenced to hang at the same time were reprieved at the last minute.

All the convicts in the settlement, male and female, were brought out to witness this event. The convict who had been appointed as hangman at first refused to perform the task. He finally cooperated, only after an officer directed the marines to shoot him if he continued to refuse. Arthur Bowes, who was a surgeon on the *Lady Penrhyn*, described the execution in his diary, referring to Barrett as 'a most vile character'.

Barrett, who had sailed on the *Charlotte*, had already drawn attention to himself. He had been caught in Rio de Janeiro trying to use some coins that he had forged during the voyage from old buttons, buckles and spoons. The coins were so expertly made that the fact that they were forged was almost impossible to detect. John White, the chief surgeon on the *Charlotte*, disapproved of Barrett's behaviour, but still expressed his 'high opinion' of Barrett's 'ingenuity, cunning [and] caution'. He wrote of his 'inexpressible surprise' that Barrett was able to melt down his materials and reshape them without being detected by officers or marines. He then wrote of his regret that Barrett's obvious skills had not been used to better advantage.

EARLY DAYS IN THE SETTLEMENT

As you already read on the opposite page, young Thomas Barrett was hanged for stealing food barely three weeks after the First Fleet arrived in Sydney Cove. A shortage of food plagued the new settlement for the first few years of its existence. The First Fleet had taken on animals, agricultural equipment and seeds for crops during the month it stopped at Cape Town. But until farms had been established and crops grown, the only food available were the supplies on board ship and the fish and animals that could be caught and hunted. Of course, the Aborigines who lived around the harbour knew how to gather edible native plants, fruits and berries, but the newcomers at first had no knowledge of what was suitable to eat.

Even though there was enough food on the First Fleet to feed the people of the new colony for up to two years, this food was not very healthy, and it had to be severely rationed. Each week, the rations were handed out at the public store. Sailors, marines and officers each received about 2 kilograms of beef and 1 kilogram of pork per week, as well as a small amount of dried peas, butter, oatmeal and vinegar. The male convicts were given only about two-thirds of this ration and the female convicts received two-thirds of the male convict ration. This was enough to keep most of the convicts alive but it was not enough to keep many of them healthy. Because convicts ate very little fresh fruit or vegetables, many of them suffered from a disease called scurvy. Scurvy was common in those days when people spent long periods at sea. Dysentery, which is a kind of food poisoning, was also common, especially among the convicts.

Fortunately, the early settlers did find some plants that proved useful in treating scurvy. Late in 1788, a female convict wrote of a 'kind of chickweed so much in taste like our spinach that no difference can be discerned'. She had also tasted kangaroo, which she described as 'like mutton, but much leaner'. Some vegetables were grown on an island in Sydney Harbour, which is now called Garden Island. This made it difficult for hungry convicts or marines to steal them. The red sap of one of the native gum trees proved to be effective in treating cases of dysentery.

An official document signed in late September 1788 by David Collins, the chief law officer of the

Aborigines were skilled at hunting and gathering food. The white settlers struggled in their new environment.

colony, gives us a good idea of how much worse off the convicts were than the soldiers. It shows that a total of 56 people had died since coming ashore in January. Of these, 51 were convicts or the children of convicts. Thirty male convicts were among the dead—four of these had been hanged. Twelve female convicts and nine children of convicts had died in these first eight months of white settlement. One woman and 11 men had escaped and were still missing. These figures can be explained to some extent by the fact that when they arrived in Sydney about one out of three male convicts was too ill to be put to work.

Almost two years later, in July 1790, the condition of the convicts was even worse. A survey taken at that time shows that out of 729 male convicts in Sydney, only 316 were employed in any kind of work. The rest—well over half of them—were being treated for illness.

Convicts at work

Almost immediately after coming ashore in Sydney Town, those convicts who were not too weak or ill were put to work. In the early months of the new settlement, land had to be cleared, buildings put up and crops grown. One of the problems in employing convicts in these jobs was that most of them had very few work skills and very little inclination to work. Many of them who had lived by thieving or begging had no previous experience of productive work. In May 1788 Phillip complained about the lack of carpenters in the colony. There were only 12 convict carpenters and several of those were too sick to work. He also wrote that few of the convicts 'are inclined to be industrious . . . and we have many who are helpless and are a dead-weight on the settlement'.

The new settlement urgently needed buildings. Even though it was high summer when the fleet arrived and the weather was warm, there were frequent thunderstorms and heavy rain squalls in the first couple of weeks. The canvas tents in which everyone was first housed had to be replaced with more solid and permanent dwellings. This meant that trees had to be felled for building timber, and within days of their arrival teams of convicts, directed by the surveyor-general, Augustus Alt, were at work felling trees. The early huts were crude constructions that became known as wattle-and-daub buildings. They consisted of vertical poles with pieces of bark and caked mud between them. The roofs were a kind of thatch made of reeds. Later on, more substantial buildings were constructed of crude bricks made of local clay. A convict, who had been a brickmaker in England, supervised the making of these bricks. Later still, many of the settlement's important buildings were constructed with sandstone, which was plentiful in the Sydney region.

Many of the convict work gangs were supervised by other convicts, called overseers. These overseers, who were selected because they were thought to be well-behaved and reliable, were often greatly disliked by the convicts who worked under them. The overseers were the first convicts in the colony

The first Government House was built on a rise just above Sydney Cove. This is where Jane Dundas (see pages 30–31) was first 'assigned'.

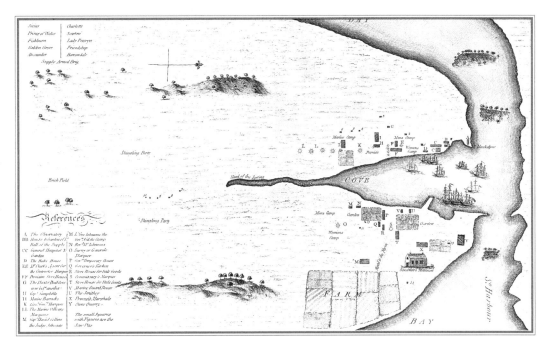

This plan of Sydney was drawn by a convict, Francis Fowkes, on 16 April 1788. You can see clearly the farm that was already established where the Botanic Gardens are today.

to be given any kind of authority. As time went by, more convicts would be put in positions of responsibility. Some even acted as prison guards or policemen.

Other convicts were given the job of making farms so that crops could be grown. The first farm in the colony was established on part of what is now the Sydney Botanic Gardens. This was back-breaking work. First of all, the land had to be cleared and the ground ploughed up by hand using axes and hoes. There were no ploughs in the early settlement and, in any case, there were no horses to pull them. The first attempts to grow crops were very dispiriting, both for the convict workers and the officers and other officials. The soil in Sydney turned out to be poor and ants and other pests attacked the crops. By September 1788, Phillip realised that farming in Sydney was not going to work. He wrote in his report to the British government that 'very little of the English wheat had vegetated, and a very considerable quantity of barley and many seeds had rotted in the ground . . . All the barley and wheat which had been put on board the Supply at the Cape were destroyed by the weevil'.

At first the convicts were made to work 10 hours per day from Monday to Friday and for six hours on Saturday mornings. However, in 1789 and 1790 convicts were allowed to stop work at three o'clock in the afternoon so that they could grow their own food. By this time food was becoming seriously scarce in the colony. No ships bringing new supplies of food arrived in Sydney during 1788 or 1789. The British government had sent a ship, the *Guardian*, during 1789, but it had been wrecked near Cape Town and all its supplies were lost.

Women at work

Finding useful employment for the women convicts in the early settlement posed a problem for the governor and other officials. In July 1790 Phillip wrote in a tone of resignation: 'I do not reckon on the little labour that may be got from the women', and the following year a Dr John Harris wrote in a letter home to England that the women convicts were 'a useless burthen to this colony, no work being fit to put them to consequently they do nothing'.

There is no doubt that the behaviour of many women convicts was disruptive. Drunkenness was a problem. Even though they were not given alcohol as part of their rations, many women were able to get rum from seamen or marines with whom they formed relationships. On the night of 6 February 1788, the day the women convicts were first brought ashore, there were riotous scenes on the shores of Sydney Cove as the male convicts and seamen from the ships swarmed into the women's tents. In the middle of this wild party a violent summer storm hit the settlement, bringing down a large gum tree and killing five sheep and a pig. The partying convicts seemed not to notice the weather. As Arthur Bowes wrote in his diary: 'The scene which presented itself . . . during the greater part of the night beggars every description. Some swearing, some quarrelling, some singing—not in the least regarding the tempest.' The next morning Phillip sternly warned the assembled convicts that such behaviour would not be tolerated in future.

As we have seen, some women had children with them when they arrived; others gave birth after arriving. By December 1788, 28 babies who had been born in the colony had been christened. Looking after these children was a full-time occupation for a number of convict women. Even women who had no children of their own were sometimes given the job of looking after children. For example, in October 1788, Susannah Allen died while giving birth to a baby daughter, so another convict woman, Frances Davis, was given the child to take care of. The baby's father, a private in the marines, either could not or did not want to care for her. Unfortunately the child, Rebecca Allen, also died just over three months later.

Other convict women were employed doing some of the lighter work involved in clearing land and making gardens. Many were sent off to scour the rocks around the shoreline for oyster shells that could be ground up to make mortar for the buildings. Until Mary Bryant made her escape, which you read about on page 25, she had

been employed picking native sarsaparilla leaves that were used to make a kind of tea. She even managed to take a packet of these leaves to England with her and presented it to James Boswell, a prominent writer who was one of the people who pleaded for her to be pardoned.

A number of women were given the job of making and mending clothes, both for themselves and for the male convicts and marines. In September 1788, Phillip established a new settlement west of Sydney at Rose Hill. It is now called Parramatta. Here the soil was much richer than the soil in the Sydney region and Phillip hoped that farms around Rose Hill would be more successful at producing crops than the farms that had been established in Sydney. At the end of 1791, there were 133 women convicts in the Rose Hill area. Most of them were put to work making shirts, trousers and other items of clothing for the male convicts.

A few of the First Fleet women convicts were 'assigned' to act as servants in the huts or houses of military officers or high-ranking officials. One of these was 30-year-old laundrymaid Jane Dundas, who had been sentenced the previous year to seven years transportation for stealing linen from her employer. It was her first offence and at her trial the household

An early scene at Rose Hill, which was later named Parramatta.

butler had described her as being of 'good character' and 'a very sober girl'. She sailed on the *Prince of Wales*, where she formed a relationship with one of the ship's officers. No doubt because of this connection, she became the housekeeper for Governor Phillip. When Phillip returned to England in 1792, she stayed on as housekeeper, first to Major Francis Grose and then to Captain William Paterson, the two army officers who governed the colony until 1795, when Governor Hunter arrived to take over. In 1796, she was a free woman and returned to England. She returned to Sydney as a free settler in 1800 and became housekeeper for another governor, Philip Gidley King. She died in 1805, and King attended her funeral. He even had a headstone placed over her grave, expressing his sorrow at losing a loyal and faithful servant.

Many female convicts, like the one here, were assigned to work as servants in the homes of free settlers.

'Assigned' convicts

Jane Dundas was one of the first convicts to be 'assigned' to work for a particular person. As the colony gradually grew larger and expanded further afield, many convicts were assigned to work for individual employers—often free settlers, but frequently ex-convicts who had served their term and now had their freedom—on their farms or properties. Convicts, both male and female, worked as servants. Many male convicts were assigned as shepherds on pastoral properties or as labourers on farms. This system suited the landholders, because, although they had to feed and clothe their convict labourers, they did not have to pay them for their work. It also suited the authorities

because it saved them the cost of feeding and housing convicts.

The survey of male convicts that was taken in July 1790 shows that 38 convicts in Sydney were 'employed by the officers of the civil and military departments at their farms'. Ten years later, there were almost ten times that number of assigned convicts. By 1825, the number of convicts assigned to private individuals had risen to almost 11 000.

Many convicts, especially those assigned to 'masters' who treated them fairly, did well out of the assignment system. There were rules that spelt out the number of hours a convict could be required to work. After about 1804, assigned convicts were allowed to work longer hours and to be paid for the extra time they worked. Not surprisingly, though, other convicts found themselves working for unreasonable, and often cruel, employers who tried to work them excessively hard and to save money by cutting back on their rations and clothing allowances.

An early success story

One of Sydney's best known high schools is James Ruse Agricultural High School. Every student in Years 7 to 10 at this school takes Agriculture as one of their subjects and gains some practical experience of farming methods. This school is named after one of the most famous of the First Fleet convicts.

James Ruse was a farmer in Cornwall, England. In 1782, at the age of 22, he was found guilty of breaking and entering and sentenced to seven years transportation. For

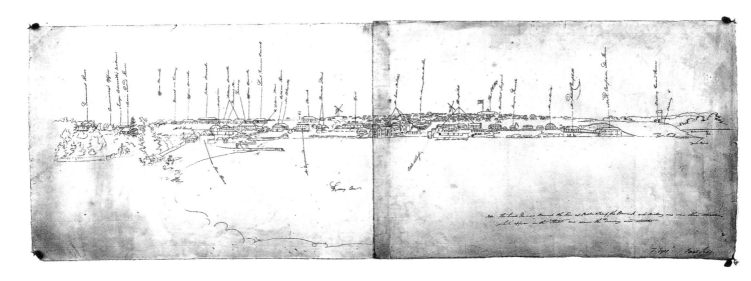

A pencil sketch showing the growing town of Sydney in 1809.

the next five years, he languished in prison and on board a prison hulk at Plymouth. He sailed to New South Wales on the *Scarborough*. In July 1789, his sentence expired and he was given his freedom. Phillip, who was now desperate to develop successful farms in the colony, offered Ruse a deal. If Ruse agreed to stay in the colony, he would be given two acres (almost a hectare) of land at Rose Hill in order to set up a farm. If Ruse could show that he could support himself on the produce of this farm, Phillip promised to give him a much larger grant of 12 hectares. Ruse agreed to this deal, and so became the first person in the colony to be given a grant of land.

The deal that Phillip offered Ruse was an experiment. In fact, the small farm that Ruse was given was named Experiment Farm. After the early unsuccessful attempts at raising crops in Sydney, many people in the colony were feeling pessimistic. They claimed that it was not possible to make farms work in New South Wales. Phillip wanted to use James Ruse to prove them wrong. Ruse did not let him down.

With the help of a single assigned convict, Ruse cleared and prepared the ground for cultivation. As there was no animal manure to fertilise the soil, he burnt the trees that he cut down and worked the ashes into the ground. He then carefully turned the soil, a little bit at a time, using a hand-held hoe.

As he later said, it was 'not like the government farm, just scratched over, but properly done'. Next he dug in grass and weeds in order to make the soil richer. It was arduous work, but it produced results. By early 1791, he was able to show that he could support himself entirely from the produce of his farm. By the end of the year, he was able to support his wife and child as well. Ruse married Elizabeth Perry, a convict woman, during 1790. After he married, the convict who was assigned to help Ruse was taken away and Ruse and his wife worked the farm entirely by themselves.

Ruse prospered from his hard work. In 1792, Phillip, true to his word, granted him the promised 12 hectares, at a place not far from the original farm. The following year, Ruse sold this to a free settler, Surgeon John Harris. In 1798, Harris built a handsome stone cottage on this farm. He called it Experiment Farm Cottage. The cottage, restored to its original condition, is still standing and is open to the public for inspection.

James Ruse lived a prosperous life after he sold his farm. He died in 1837. Part of the inscription on his tombstone claims that he 'sowd the Forst Grain'. That is not strictly true, but he was the first farmer to show that agriculture in New South Wales could, with hard work and proper care, be made to work. Ruse's was one of the first great success stories among the Australian convicts.

THE SECOND FLEET

While James Ruse was busy working his farm at Rose Hill, the colony was quickly running out of food. In April 1790, in an attempt to preserve food, Phillip cut the convicts' weekly rations to just under one-and-a-half kilograms of flour, just under one kilogram of salted meat and just under one kilogram of rice. So that convicts could not eat their entire ration at once, only half this food was given out at a time. On this kind of diet, many convicts became too ill to work. Some, desperately hungry, stole from gardens and farms. One hungry convict, Joseph Elliott, was caught stealing a few potatoes from the garden of the chaplain, Richard Johnson. He was given 300 lashes (a sentence that would have left his back almost bare of skin), then chained to two other convicts in a work gang for six months. His ration of flour was stopped for six months. A few days later, Phillip changed his mind about stopping the man's flour ration. Without it, he would probably have died.

A number of convicts did die from hunger or from diseases that resulted from their poor diet. In May 1790, an elderly convict collapsed from hunger while waiting to collect his ration. He died the next day. It turned out that the poor man had lost his cooking pot and his fellow convicts had refused to let him use theirs unless he gave them some of his food. As a result he grew weaker. Eventually he took to eating his rice uncooked. As he was unable to digest the uncooked rice, he became even more ill and eventually died of hunger.

Not long after, on the afternoon of 3 June 1790, there was great excitement in Sydney Town as the news quickly spread that a ship had sailed into the harbour. The excitement soon turned to disappointment when this ship, the *Lady Juliana*, proved to be the first of

Farewell to Black-Eyed Sue and Sweet Poll of Plymouth. *This cartoon, published in the 1790s, shows two convicts saying farewell to their tearful sweethearts.*

a new fleet of convict ships. It brought 222 women convicts and some provisions, but not enough to make much difference in the colony. The *Lady Juliana* was part of what is now known as the Second Fleet. However, unlike the ships of the First Fleet, the six ships of the Second Fleet left England at different times. The *Lady Juliana* had been the first to leave and had taken just over 10 months to make the journey.

Conditions on board

Over the next four weeks, four more ships arrived in Sydney. The first of them was welcome indeed. It was the *Justinian*, which brought no new convicts, but was laden with much-needed provisions. The remaining three ships—the *Surprize*, the *Neptune* and the *Scarborough*— were transport ships bringing, between them, about 1100 convicts, including about 90 women. The *Scarborough* was a First Fleet ship making its second voyage to the colony.

The women convicts on the *Lady Juliana* were generally in reasonable health after their long voyage. The ship had followed the same route as the ships of the First Fleet. It had spent seven weeks in Rio de Janeiro and a month at the Cape of Good Hope. (It was at the Cape that the people on board the *Lady Juliana* learned that the *Guardian*, the supply ship that you read about on page 29, had been wrecked by an iceberg.) The British government had sent a naval officer on the *Lady Juliana* to ensure that the convicts were properly fed and were able to wash regularly. As a result, only three convicts and one child had died during the voyage. Several babies were born to convict women during the voyage. One woman from this ship later wrote in a letter that the babies 'had great care taken of them, and baby linen and every necessary for them were ready made to be put on'.

The four other transports told a dramatically different story. On these ships the convicts had endured great hardships. They were kept chained together below decks for most of the time in terribly overcrowded spaces. Even though enough food was provided for the

voyage, the guards kept most of it from the convicts. Often, when one convict died from sickness or starvation, the other convicts who were chained to him would hide the fact from the guards so that they could eat his rations. One convict later described how he ate his dead comrade's food for a week before the dead body was discovered.

It is hardly surprising, then, that a total of 256 convicts died on the voyage. The worst ship was the *Neptune*. It was the largest, but by far the most crowded, of the ships. One hundred and fifty-eight out of the 502 convicts who sailed on this ship died on the journey. Of about 850 convicts who survived the voyage, almost 500 were desperately ill. They were taken straight to the hospital tents on the shores of Sydney Cove. More than 120 of these died soon after.

The Reverend Richard Johnson watched in horror as the convicts came ashore. He described the grim scene in his diary: '. . . many were not able to walk, to stand, or to stir themselves in the least . . . Some creeped upon their hands and knees, and some were carried upon the backs of others.' When he visited them later in the hospital tents, he found that 'many were not able to turn or even to stir themselves, and . . . were covered over almost with their own nastiness, their heads, bodies, cloths, blankets, all full of filth and lice'.

Why was the voyage of the Second Fleet so much worse than the voyage of the First Fleet? It was mainly because the British government had contracted a private company to ship the convicts to New South Wales. This company was paid an amount of money for each convict. The amount of money was the same whether the convict lived or died. In order to save money, the crews starved the convicts. So that there was no chance of a rebellion, they kept their charges chained below decks. In order to make as much money as possible, they crowded the convicts into as few ships as possible. Crew members from the ships were able to make extra money by selling the food they kept back from the convicts.

The Soldiers' Farewell. *Soldiers bound for New South Wales farewell their wives and children.*

when they arrived, and many died soon after. One of these ships, the *Queen*, brought 222 male convicts to Sydney. Less than a year after arriving, 172 of these had died. According to one report, the convicts on the *Queen* had been issued with less than half the meat rations they were supposed to receive during the voyage. The same shipowners who were responsible for the Second Fleet provided the ships and crews for the Third Fleet. Once again, complaints were made to the authorities in Britain. Once again, nothing was done to bring offenders to trial.

Phillip wrote to the British government, complaining about the condition of the convicts on the Second Fleet. Some crew members on the *Neptune* also made complaints about the ship's captain, Donald Trail. They claimed that he was responsible for the deaths of several convicts. There was an inquiry, but no-one was brought to trial.

A Third Fleet

It would be just over a year after the last ship of the Second Fleet sailed into Port Jackson before another ship from England would arrive. On 9 July 1791, the *Mary Anne* arrived after a voyage of about six months. Over the next three months, nine more ships would arrive. This Third Fleet, as it became known, brought with it almost 1900 convicts, all but about 170 of them male. About 180 convicts had died during the voyage.

While conditons for convicts on board the ships of the Third Fleet were better than on the Second Fleet, they were still very poor. More than one-quarter of the convicts on these ships were seriously ill

Changes, however, were made. For one thing, the shipowners of the Second and Third fleets were given no more contracts to bring convicts to New South Wales. All future convict ships were supposed to have a qualified doctor on board to look after the health of the convicts. As well, private shipowners were paid extra for transporting convicts who were still alive when they arrived in New South Wales. For some time, the situation improved dramatically. Then, after 1795, when Britain went to war with France, there were no naval doctors available to sail to New South Wales and more convicts died on the voyages. However, the Second Fleet and, to a lesser extent, the Third Fleet, had taught the British authorities a lesson. Conditions on future convict ships were never as bad again.

A NEW SETTLEMENT

An area of Sydney on the shores of Botany Bay is known as La Perouse. It is named after the famous French explorer, Jean-François de la Pérouse, whose two ships, *La Boussole* and *L'Astrolobe*, sailed into Botany Bay on 24 January 1788, just as the ships of the First Fleet were preparing to sail north to Port Jackson. La Pérouse was leading a voyage of discovery in the South Pacific, and had heard that the British were planning to establish a colony in Botany Bay.

Phillip was already in Port Jackson when the French ships came into Botany Bay. Captain Hunter of the *Sirius* sent a sailor to carry greetings to the French captain and then set sail as quickly as possible for Port Jackson. Even though courtesies were exchanged, the British officers were suspicious of La Pérouse and told him very little about where they were about to establish their settlement.

No doubt the convicts on the transport ships also saw the French ships, and some of them probably decided on the spot to use them as a means of escape. A few days later, a number of male convicts stole away from the settlement on Sydney Cove and somehow managed to find their way through the bush to Botany Bay. They went on board *La Boussole* and offered their services as crewmen. La Pérouse angrily sent them away, but he gave them some food so that they could get back safely to Sydney Cove. A few returned, but some remained at large, possibly lost in the bush. Those that returned were the first convicts to be flogged in the new colony.

If La Pérouse had taken them on board, they would have been dead within a couple of months. The two French ships stayed for six weeks in Botany Bay, and then sailed northeast. They were wrecked near one of the islands that are now called Vanuatu. All on board died.

A quick decision

On Saturday 2 February 1788, Phillip sent Captain Philip Gidley King to Botany Bay to meet La Pérouse. The French explorer treated

Jean-François de la Pérouse.

King very courteously. The day before, however, King had already written in his diary: 'This day His Excellency Governor Phillip signified his intention of sending me to Norfolk Island with a few people to stock and settle it. Lieutenant Ball of the Supply was ordered to receive the stores on board necessary for that purpose.' Phillip wanted to make certain that he claimed Norfolk Island as part of the new colony before the French could get there and claim it.

At six o'clock in the evening of 14 February, the *Sirius* sailed out of Sydney Harbour bound for Norfolk Island. On board were King, who was to be the commandant of the new settlement, another naval officer, nine male convicts, six female convicts, a surgeon and assistant surgeon, two seamen and two marines. Also on board were some sheep, pigs and poultry, as well as seeds, plants and tools for farming and enough provisions to feed the pioneers of the new settlement for six months. Three weeks later, the *Supply* completed its 1500-kilometre voyage and landed its cargo of people, animals and provisions at a spot on the island where the town of Kingston now stands.

Norfolk Island is now a pleasant South Pacific holiday destination, where visitors enjoy the magnificent coastal scenery and wander around what remains of the old convict settlement. But it was a far from pleasant place for most of the convicts who were sent there. It was in many ways the perfect prison. Its isolated location and its steep cliffs and dangerous seas made escape almost impossible. The 23 people who formed the first settlement would see the population of the island grow to about 1000 over the next four years.

Right from the start, life was difficult for the newcomers. The soil proved to be rich and fertile, but clearing the land for farming was slow and difficult work and most of the early plantings were attacked by rats, insects or birds. Convicts often had to work with almost empty stomachs. Fish were plentiful in the waters around the island but high seas and the surrounding rocky reefs meant that it was often too dangerous for the two small boats that were left on the island to venture out.

Discipline, too, was often harsh here. You read on page 23 how young John Hudson was given 50 lashes for the relatively minor offence of being outside his hut after dark. In 1792, John Easty, a marine, visited the island briefly and described it as a 'poor miserable place' where floggings were common and were sometimes so brutal that the victim died as a result. He described King as a 'tyrant' who behaved 'more like a mad man than a man trusted with

Philip Gidley King, the first commandant of Norfolk Island.

the government of an island . . . belonging to Great Britain'.

However, the convicts on Norfolk Island suffered much worse between 1800 and 1804, when an officer of the New South Wales Corps, Major Joseph Foveaux, became lieutenant-governor of the island. Foveaux was described by one of the officials who worked for him on the island as a 'hard and determined' man who believed 'more in the lash than in the Bible'. The same man later wrote that Foveaux enjoyed watching convicts being flogged. Sometimes, when the punishment was completed he would force the victim, who was now in agony and with his back almost bare of skin and covered with blood, to go straight back to work.

About five months after he arrived, Foveaux was told by a convict of a plot by some other convicts to revolt against their guards and kill them with sharpened sticks. Soldiers immediately searched the convicts' quarters and discovered the weapons. Foveaux did not bother with a trial or a hearing. The two ringleaders of the revolt were immediately arrested and were hanged the same night.

Women on Norfolk Island

As you read on page 13, the British government wanted to colonise Norfolk Island largely because of the flax that grew there. This, they thought, could be used to make sails and ropes for British ships. Many women convicts were sent to Norfolk Island in the early years. Most of the women convicts who arrived on the *Lady Juliana* in March 1790 left again in the same ship when it sailed to Norfolk Island on its way to China at the end of July. Only a few days later, another of the Second Fleet ships, the *Surprize*, sailed for Norfolk Island, taking 150 female convicts and 30 male convicts.

Many of the women convicts were employed on the island producing cloth for ships' sails from the flax plants that grew there. By the early 1800s, however, it had become obvious that they would not be able to produce a worthwhile amount of cloth. Only one ship ever sailed with sails made from Norfolk Island flax. The beautiful pines that are still a feature of the island were also a disappointment. The wood proved too soft for making ships' masts. Because of these problems, and the cost of maintaining a settlement so far from Sydney, fewer and fewer convicts were sent to the island. When Governor Lachlan Macquarie arrived in the colony in 1810, there were only 117 convicts there. Eventually, in 1814, the convict settlement was abandoned and the island was given over to free settlers.

Ten years later these free settlers were removed and Norfolk Island began its second era as a convict settlement—this time as a 'place of secondary punishment'.

A view of Norfolk Island in about 1812, not long before the convict settlement there was abandoned. You can see clearly how parts of the hillsides had been cleared of their pine trees.

CONVICTS AND THE NEW SOUTH WALES CORPS

As well as convicts, the Second Fleet brought some new soldiers to the colony. These were the first contingent of the New South Wales Corps, a military group that was formed especially to preserve order and supervise the convicts in New South Wales. They were to replace the marines, who sailed to the colony with the First Fleet. Officers of the New South Wales Corps would soon become very powerful in the colony and would strongly influence the way the convicts lived and worked.

When Phillip left the colony to return to England late in 1792, the job of governing the colony was taken over first by Major Francis Grose and then by Captain William Paterson. They ruled the colony until the next governor, John Hunter, arrived in 1795. Even after Governor Hunter arrived, the officers of the New South Wales Corps had become so powerful that it was difficult for the governor to control them. Between 1792 and 1810, the New South Wales Corps, and not the governor, was the real power in the colony. In 1808, officers of the New South Wales Corps arrested the governor, William Bligh, kept him prisoner for two weeks and then forced him to leave the colony. Major George Johnston then declared himself lieutenant-governor and ruled the colony for the next two years.

You read on page 32 how, in July 1789, the former convict James Ruse became the first person to receive a grant of land in New South Wales. In the following three years, 53 more convicts who had completed their sentences (these people were known as 'emancipists') were given grants of land. Even though most convicts had received sentences of seven years or more, some had already served several years in prison before being transported.

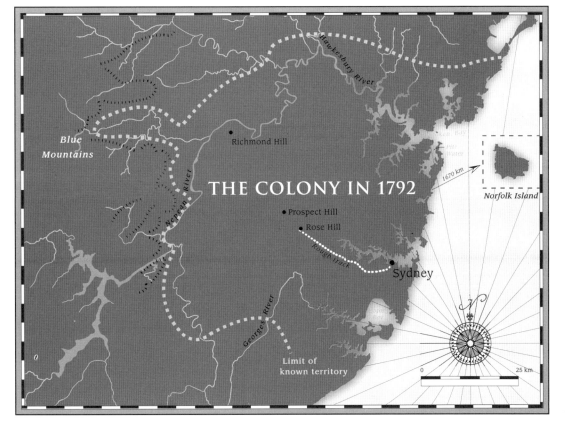

THE COLONY IN 1792

The Colony in 1792, when Phillip left. The area outside the dotted line had not yet been visited by white settlers. It is possible, though, that some escaped convicts may have moved further afield.

A cartoon showing members of the New South Wales Corps arresting Governor Bligh in 1808.

Phillip made these land grants to emancipists for two main reasons. First, he wanted to encourage these former convicts to stay on in the colony as free settlers. Second, he wanted them to set up farms so that they could feed themselves and their families and contribute food to the colony as a whole. Most of these grants were in the Parramatta region and further west around Toongabbie, where the soil had proved to be suitable for agriculture. The grants were of 30 acres (12 hectares). To encourage emancipists to marry and have children, Phillip gave married emancipists an extra 20 acres (8 hectares). They could also receive an extra 10 acres (4 hectares) for every child they had. Phillip did not believe that marines or officers should receive land grants.

After Phillip left, the situation changed. Many more grants of land were made. Some of these were made to emancipists, but others were made to officers of the New South Wales Corps. The new rulers of the colony—first Grose and then Paterson—had little sympathy for convicts or emancipists. According to Grose, the officers were the 'only description of settlers on whom reliance can be placed'. He therefore gave preference to the officers over the emancipists by granting land to any officer who wanted it. Most officers received grants of 25 acres (10 hectares), but many were granted 100 acres (40 hectares), often in the most fertile areas. As well as the land, each officer was given, free of charge, the services of 10 convicts. This greatly expanded the assignment system that you read about on page 31. Major Grose also changed the rules about rations. Under Phillip, convicts and soldiers were entitled to the same rations. Under Grose, convicts' rations were reduced and they received less than soldiers did.

Governor William Bligh.

Officers, convicts and rum

Most of the troubles between the governors and the officers of the New South Wales Corps were about rum. Right from the beginning of the colony, rum had been the main form of alcohol in New South Wales. Convicts were not given rum, but many managed to get it by giving part of their rations to marines and sailors in exchange for some of the precious drink. Not surprisingly, drinking rum and eating even less food than usual badly affected the health of many convicts and made it more difficult for them to work.

Soon after Phillip left, the officers of the New South Wales Corps combined to purchase a huge amount of rum from a visiting American ship. They really had very little choice, because the captain of the ship would not sell any of the other much-needed provisions he had on board unless he could also sell all of the rum the ship was carrying. As a result, the officers now had complete control of the supply of rum in the colony, and they maintained this monopoly over the rum supply for the next 15 years. It was not long before rum became the main means of paying for goods and labour in the colony. There was very little real money in the colony and even though officers had convicts assigned to work on their farms, they needed more help. Grose allowed some convicts to work on the officers' farms for part of every day in return for payment. The officers paid these convicts by giving them rum. Many convicts who worked in this way refused to accept any other form of payment.

First Governor Hunter, and then Philip Gidley King, who replaced him as governor in 1800, tried to outlaw the use of rum as a form of currency and payment for labour, but the custom was too well established and the army officers too powerful. When Bligh replaced King in 1806, he was determined to stamp out the trade in rum. He too failed and, as we saw, was arrested and sent out of the colony by the officers of the New South Wales Corps. This action by the New South Wales Corps became known as the Rum Rebellion.

Emancipist farmers

Many of the early emancipist farmers did not make a success of their farms, especially in the early days of the colony. One reason is that, unlike James Ruse, very few of them had any previous experience of farming or knowledge of farming methods. Most of them were poor and unable to afford proper farming equipment. The army officers who were granted land had a huge advantage over them. As you read earlier, they had free convict labour and many of them could get convicts who had been farmers before they were transported. The officers, too, generally had larger farms and were able to grow a greater variety of crops and raise a larger number of farm animals.

In 1795, there were just over 250 emancipist farmers in the colony. Five years later, only about 90 of these were still farming their land. Almost 20 years later, however—in 1819—the number of emancipist farmers had risen to 857. Between them, they farmed a total of about 17 000 hectares. At the same time, there were just over 200 officers and other free settlers who owned farms. Their farms were, on average, almost 20 times as large as those of the emancipist farmers.

John Macarthur

In 1819, John Macarthur was one of the largest landowners and one of the most successful farmers in the colony. During the 1790s, Macarthur had been one of the first people to breed merino sheep in the colony, and he is often referred to as the father of Australia's wool industry.

Macarthur came to the colony with the Second Fleet in 1790 as an officer of the New South Wales Corps. He soon became one of the most powerful men in the colony. As paymaster for the New South Wales Corps, he was able to arrange for the officers to make purchases of rum, and as inspector of public works, he was able to arrange to have a small army of convicts working on his properties. Macarthur was a quarrelsome man who clashed with a succession of governors. In

During Macarthur's long absence from the colony, his wife, Elizabeth Macarthur, ran his properties, which included large areas now in the Camden area, which was then known as Cowpastures, as well as landholdings in Parramatta. When Macarthur returned to the colony, Lachlan Macquarie had been governor for seven years. Macarthur very soon came into conflict with Macquarie, mainly because he felt the governor was too sympathetic to convicts and too generous in his attempts to help emancipists become prosperous and make useful contributions to the colony.

Macarthur was no friend to either convicts or ex-convicts. He hated seeing them do well and he began writing letters to influential friends in England, complaining that Macquarie was giving them favourable treatment. Unlike Macquarie, Macarthur believed that convicts deserved to be punished for their crimes, even after they had served their sentences and proved themselves to be good, hard-working citizens. They should not be encouraged or allowed to consider themselves the equals of army officers or of people who had arrived in the colony as free settlers. The people who received Macarthur's letters soon began to plot Macquarie's downfall.

Captain John Macarthur.

1801, Governor King sent him back to England to stand trial after he was involved in a duel with his superior officer. In 1808, he plotted the Rum Rebellion, which ended in Governor Bligh's arrest and departure from the colony. In 1809, fearing that the next governor would arrest him for his part in the Rum Rebellion, Macarthur sailed back to England. He remained there until 1817, when he was given permission to return to the colony.

Elizabeth Farm, Macarthur's first farm at Parramatta. Macarthur had the help of many convict labourers in developing this farm and his other properties.

CONVICTS IN THE MACQUARIE ERA

Governor Lachlan Macquarie.

When Lachlan Macqaurie officially became governor of New South Wales, it was in many ways the beginning of a new era for the colony. For one thing, it marked the end of the power of the New South Wales Corps. When Macquarie arrived, he brought with him a new regiment, the 73rd Regiment, to enforce law and order. The New South Wales Corps was disbanded and about half its members soon returned to England. The rest remained. Some joined the new regiment; the others became part of a special Veteran Corps which Macquarie set up.

For the next 10 years it would be Macquarie who mainly controlled what went on in the colony. Macquarie made many enemies while he was governor, but they were mainly powerful free settlers. During Macquarie's term as governor, life for many convicts

improved. Macquarie wanted to develop a colony in which people, both free settlers and convicts, could lead full and contented lives. Previously, convicts were regarded mainly as people to be punished for their crimes. Macquarie believed that being transported was punishment enough. Unless they committed new crimes in the colony, convicts should enjoy the same rights and privileges as other free settlers once their sentences had expired. He also believed in rewarding good behaviour by issuing convicts tickets of leave, or even pardons, before they had served their full sentences. Having a ticket of leave was a bit like being on bail. It meant that the convict was free to work for pay within a particular area, as long as he or she reported regularly to a magistrate. If the convict misbehaved or committed an offence, they could lose their ticket of leave—and their freedom. Such ideas brought Macquarie into conflict with many

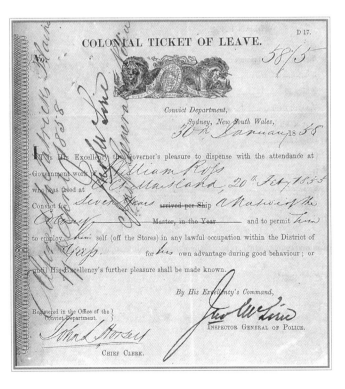

A ticket of leave.

Dr William Redfern.

influential and wealthy free settlers. These settlers, who became known as 'exclusives', resented any rights and privileges enjoyed by ex-convicts, or 'emancipists'.

The exclusives, for example, were unhappy when Macquarie, very soon after his arrival, invited three emancipists to dine with him. They were William Redfern, who was assistant surgeon of the colony; Andrew Thompson, a farmer; and Simeon Lord, a trader and businessman. Also present was D'Arcy Wentworth, who had twice been tried for highway robbery in England but had not been convicted. He sailed to New South Wales with the Second Fleet as a surgeon and was chief surgeon of the colony in 1810. Although he was not an ex-convict, the exclusives regarded him as being as bad as one. These four men were now rich and successful, but were still not accepted by the exclusives. The exclusives were even more unhappy when, soon afterwards, Macquarie appointed Thompson and Simeon Lord as magistrates, who could try and sentence both convicts and free settlers who were accused of crimes. Thompson died soon after, and Macquarie further offended many free settlers by being the chief mourner at his funeral.

During Macquarie's time, great changes took place in the colony. The town of Sydney, which was a ramshackle collection of buildings when he arrived, was a distinctly grander place when he left. Streets were straightened and widened and a number of handsome new buildings sprang up. Several of these still stand. They included a hospital, a convict barracks and St James's church. You can see these buildings at the top end of Macquarie Street.

Soon after he arrived, Macquarie visited the Hawkesbury River area, where recent floods had destroyed crops, and decided to establish new towns on higher ground. These towns, which include Richmond, Windsor and Castlereagh, still contain buildings that were built during the Macquarie era.

Convict workers and a convict architect

Convicts were still forced to work hard during Macquarie's time. Many of the roads that were needed as the colony expanded were built by convict work gangs, sometimes working in chains. The first road across the Blue Mountains to the new western settlement of Bathurst was completed early in 1815. A team

Convicts building the road across the Blue Mountains to Bathurst.

of 30 convicts took on the difficult and dangerous task, first of clearing a track through the forest and then of making the road. Parts of the road were extremely steep and along towering cliff ledges. Several convicts were killed in accidents. Those who survived the ordeal were given their freedom as a reward.

Convicts also laboured on the buildings that Macquarie had constructed in Sydney and in the new settlements. Often they worked under the supervision of an ex-convict named Francis Greenway. Greenway is probably the best example of how convicts could prosper under Macquarie's policies.

Francis Greenway had worked as an architect in England and was part owner of a stone-mason's yard. Greenway was not a good businessman and was often in financial trouble. In 1812, he was found guilty of forging a financial document. He was sentenced to death, but the sentence was commuted to transportation for 14 years. Greenway, unlike most convicts, was an educated man who had friends in high places. He arrived in Sydney with a letter written to Macquarie from the former governor John Hunter, recommending Greenway's skills as an architect.

Greenway served very little of his sentence. Very soon after he arrived, Macquarie granted him a ticket of leave. In 1815 Macquarie appointed him as an adviser on public buildings. Greenway made such an unfavourable report on the condition of Sydney's buildings that he quickly made enemies of many of the builders in the colony.

In March 1816, almost exactly two years after Greenway arrived in Sydney, Macquarie appointed him as the government architect and assistant engineer. His first job in this position was to design a lighthouse on Sydney's South Head. When the stonework for this lighthouse was completed in 1817, Macquarie was so pleased with it that he granted Greenway a pardon. He was now an emancipist. (Greenway's lighthouse is no longer there today, but another built nearby in a similar design still stands on Sydney's eastern shoreline.)

In the next few years, Greenway was extremely busy. He designed and supervised the construction of a total of 40 buildings, both in Sydney and in outlying parts of the colony. Eleven of Greenway's buildings are still standing. One of them is the convict barracks in Macquarie Street, Sydney. This was where convicts who worked for the government on public buildings and roads lived. It is now a public museum. You can visit it to find out more about how convicts in Sydney lived and worked.

This picture of Greenway's light-house on Sydney's South Head was painted in 1826.

A convict chain gang setting out to work from the convict barracks in Macquarie Street, Sydney.

Greenway was a hot-tempered man who made enemies easily. He even ended up making an enemy of Governor Macquarie by demanding extra money for the buildings he designed. When Macquarie left in February 1822, Greenway lost his job as government architect and once again became a private businessman. He had made so many enemies, however, among builders and other people in the community that very little business came his way. When he died 15 years later, in 1837, he was a poor man.

The end of the Macquarie era

As you read earlier, Governor Macquarie also made a lot of enemies because of his policies towards convicts. These enemies made sure that the British government knew how unhappy they were with the governor. Influential people in England also thought that buildings like those Greenway was designing

were far too grand and extravagant for what was supposed to be a convict settlement. In 1819, the British government sent a commissioner, John Thomas Bigge, to find out just what was happening. Bigge spent 18 months travelling around the colony, interviewing people. He took a lot of notice of what the rich settlers who disliked Macquarie had to say. He wrote a report that was very critical of Macqaurie's lenient treatment of convicts and his encouragement of emancipists.

Macquarie no doubt knew what Bigge's report would say about him. By 1821, he was a tired and sick man. He resigned as governor and returned to England early in 1822. When Bigge's report became public about a year later, Macquarie described it as a 'vile document'. A year later, on 1 July 1824, Macquarie died in London. Under the next two governors, Thomas Brisbane and Ralph Darling, life for convicts in New South Wales became much harder.

VAN DIEMEN'S LAND

Well before Governor Phillip established a colony in Sydney Cove in 1788, the authorities in Britain knew that the part of Australia that is now called Tasmania existed. But they did not know that it was a separate island. In 1642, the Dutch explorer Abel Tasman had landed on the southern coast of Tasmania. He named the land Van Diemen's Land and claimed it for Holland. Almost a century and a half later, in 1773, an English ship, the *Adventure*, commanded by Tobias Furneaux, explored parts of the southern and eastern coasts of Van Diemen's Land. The *Adventure* was one of two ships that were sent out to explore the southern oceans. The leader of this expedition was Captain James Cook, who, three years earlier, had explored and charted the eastern coast of the continent. Furneaux came upon Van Diemen's land by accident, after his ship had become separated from Cook's ship, the *Resolution*. Furneaux assumed that Van Diemen's Land was part of mainland Australia, which at that time was known as New Holland. It was not until 1798, when the explorers George Bass and Matthew Flinders sailed right around Van Diemen's Land, that people found out that it was a separate island.

You read on page 36 that Phillip sent convicts to Norfolk Island to make sure that the French did not get there first. The same idea was in the mind of Governor Philip Gidley King in 1803, when he decided to send a group of 35 convicts (including three women) and 14 officers and free settlers to found a settlement on the south-east coast of the island. French ships were sailing around and exploring the southern coasts of the continent, and King was concerned that they might try to claim Van Diemen's Land for France. He was also concerned about American whaling ships that were active in the south seas and that had landed close to where Hobart now stands. This first white settlement in Van Diemen's Land was under the command of Lieutenant John Bowen. Bowen's small party landed at a place on the banks of the Derwent River that he named Risdon Cove.

Both Governor King and the British government were still worried about the presence of French ships around the south of the Australian continent. As a result, the British government decided to set up a new convict colony in the Port Phillip area—near where Melbourne now stands. Colonel David Collins, who had come to New South Wales with the First Fleet but who had returned to England in 1796, was appointed to command the new colony. He sailed on the *Calcutta*, which was accompanied by the supply ship *Ocean*. After a six-month voyage, Collins arrived at Port Phillip on 9 October 1803, along with 299 male convicts, 50 marines and officers and a few free settlers.

Colonel David Collins.

Collins tried to establish a settlement on the east side of Port Phillip, at a place that is now called Sorrento. The site proved highly unsuitable. The soil was sandy and nothing could be grown there. The weather, too, was uncomfortably hot. Both the convicts and the marines soon became restless in these conditions. A number of convicts escaped into the bush and some were never found. Several marines who threatened to rebel were severely flogged. Collins wrote to Governor King in Sydney, complaining about the situation and was given permission to move his convicts and marines to Van Diemen's Land.

After 15 weeks at Port Phillip, Collins and his party sailed south to the Derwent. Here Collins took over command of Bowen's settlement and moved it across the river to the site of present-day Hobart. The new settlement was called Hobart Town.

A second settlement

Governor King was not satisfied that the settlement in the south of Van Diemen's Land would deter the French from settling in the north. He therefore decided to establish a new convict settlement in the north, near the mouth of the Tamar River, close to Bass Strait. He chose Lieutenant-Colonel William Paterson to command this settlement. Paterson arrived at Port Dalrymple with 74 convicts and about 60 soldiers on 11 November 1804. Many of these convicts were being transferred from Norfolk Island, where King had decided to reduce the size of the settlement. Two years later, Paterson moved his settlement further down the Tamar River to the site of present-day Launceston. Both Paterson and Collins remained in control of their separate settlements. It was not until 1812 that both were brought under the command of the Hobart settlement.

Free settlers, as well as ex-convicts, were encouraged to come to Van Diemen's Land. At first, very few came. By 1815, however, out of a total population (not including Aborigines) of almost 2000, only about one quarter were convicts. Six years later, in 1821, the total population was more than 7000 and just over half of

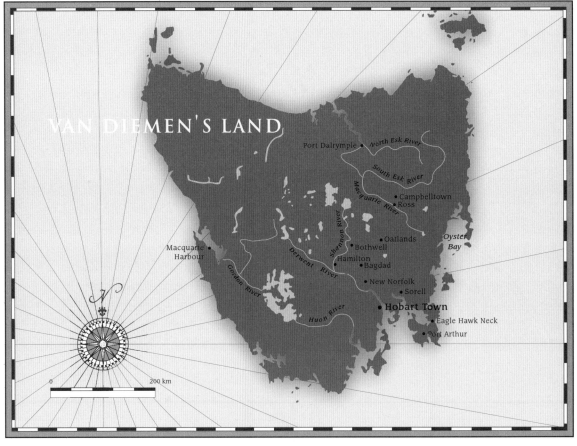

Early convict settlements in Van Diemen's Land.

Escaped convicts attacking settlers' huts.

these were convicts. Of the rest, well over half were people who had come to the island of their own accord. Many of them had been born in New South Wales. A little less than a quarter of them were emancipists (ex-convicts) and the rest were ticket-of-leave holders.

Free settlers were encouraged to come to Van Diemen's Land by being offered grants of land and the services of assigned convicts to help them develop and farm this land. By the early 1820s, 12 new settlements had been established, spreading out from Hobart Town in the south. Two new settlements had grown up in the north of the island.

As in the rest of the colony—until 1825 Van Diemen's Land was still part of New South Wales—assigned convicts had very different experiences. Some were very well treated; others were treated badly. Sometimes, close relationships developed between masters and servants. David Collins himself formed a very close friendship with James Groves, a convict who had been transported for forgery. Groves spent a great deal of time in the company of the lieutenant-governor of Hobart Town, and when Collins, at the age of 54, died suddenly

of a heart attack in 1810, Groves personally made the coffin in which his friend was buried. Groves himself died just a few weeks later.

There were, however, very few assigned convicts in the early days of Van Diemen's Land. The vast majority were employed doing 'government' work of clearing land, making roads and constructing crude buildings.

Early hardships

Just as it had been in Sydney, feeding the population soon became a major problem in Van Diemen's Land. Eagerly awaited shipments of food from Sydney failed to arrive and in 1806, floods along the Hawkesbury River, north of Sydney, destroyed wheat crops. The people in Van Diemen's Land were forced to rely on their own resources.

As food ran short, the new settlers were forced to hunt the kangaroos that were abundant in the bush surrounding the settlements. Lieutenant-Governor Collins had little choice but to issue guns to convicts so that they could hunt for food. As kangaroos and other wildlife close to the settlements were killed off, convicts had to go further afield in their search for prey.

This often brought them into conflict with groups of Aborigines. As the settlements expanded, clashes between Aboriginal groups and the new settlers became more frequent and more violent. Convicts and settlers were often speared, and Aborigines were shot dead, often on sight. Away from the settlements, a state of war existed between the new and old inhabitants.

In these circumstances, it is not surprising that many convicts took the opportunity to escape into the bush. Many survived by stealing sheep or by raiding outlying settlers' huts for food and ammunition. Others hunted and raided in groups of two or three. Often groups of escaped convicts formed larger gangs, which roamed the countryside, terrorising settlers and Aborigines. These were some of the first outbreaks of bushranging in the new colonies.

Bushrangers

After Lieutenant-Governor Collins died in 1810, he was replaced by Colonel Thomas Davey. Davey was completely incapable of controlling bushrangers and, during the seven years that he was in charge in Van Diemen's Land, the problem got much worse. It became so bad that in 1814 Lachlan Macquarie, who was now governor of New South Wales, and therefore responsible for Van Diemen's Land, ordered Davey to offer a pardon to any bushranger who surrendered before 1 December. Not many escaped convicts took advantage of this offer. Davey made a terrible example of any bushrangers who were captured by hanging them and leaving their bodies to rot in public view.

One of the best known of the convict bushrangers was Mike Howe. Howe had been transported to Sydney for highway robbery, but in 1812, he was sent to Hobart after he was convicted of a further crime. He was assigned as a servant to a merchant in Hobart, but he ran away and joined a group of bushrangers. Late in 1814, Howe took advantage of Macquarie's offer and gave himself up. Soon after, however, he escaped again and joined a gang of about 30 bushrangers led by another

escaped convict, John Whitehead. In October 1814, Whitehead was shot dead by soldiers and Howe became leader of the gang. For the next three years, Howe's gang ranged about the countryside between the two main settlements at Hobart and Launceston, raiding farms. Convicts who had been assigned as servants and workers on these farms often offered Howe and his gang help, provisions and shelter.

In 1817, Colonel William Sorell replaced Davey as Lieutenant-Governor. In that year, Howe's gang began to break up. Some of them were killed; others were captured. Howe decided to give himself up and inform on his former gang mates. In return, Sorell offered him a pardon. Howe gave evidence, not only about his convict mates, but also about a number of well-known free settlers who had bought stolen goods from them. As time went by, the official pardon failed to arrive. Howe became nervous and once again escaped. He survived for a while by raiding and robbing settlers in remote places. Eventually, in October 1818, a soldier, William Pugh, and a sailor, John Worral, tracked him to his hideout deep in the central highlands and clubbed him to death.

Other bushrangers continued to operate in Van Diemen's Land, knowing that death awaited them if they were captured. In 1821 about 20 convict bushrangers were captured and hanged in Hobart and Launceston. For several more years, convict bushrangers continued to dominate in the areas away from the main settlements.

Macquarie Harbour

Macquarie Harbour is an inlet on the south-west coast of Tasmania. To enter it, you must sail through a narrow, rocky opening known as Hell's Gates. In 1821, Lieutenant-Governor Sorel decided to establish a penal colony there. Penal colonies were also known as places of secondary punishment. They were grim places where convicts who had committed crimes since arriving in the colony were sent.

Because it was so isolated, Macquarie Harbour seemed an ideal place to send what Sorel described as the 'most disorderly and irreclaimable convicts' in Van Diemen's Land. Convicts, said Sorrel, 'must dread the very idea of being sent there'. And dread it they did. Of all the convict settlements in any of the Australian colonies, Macquarie Harbour was one of the most dreadful. Prisoners there were flogged severely for the most minor offences. A man who lost or broke one of his working tools, even if another convict stole it, could be given 50 lashes. Prisoners who were insolent could be deprived of meat and forced to work in heavy irons. One of the most feared punishments was to be kept in solitary confinement in a tiny two-roomed building on the rocky Grummet Island. Not surprisingly, Grummet Island soon became known as the Isle of the Condemned.

Most of the convicts were kept on a larger island in the harbour known as Sarah Island. Here they worked at a number of industries, including ship-building, the tanning of animal hides and timber-getting. Some of the more fortunate convicts were employed in farming vegetables and fruit to feed the settlement. Huon pine grew abundantly on the shores of Macquarie Harbour, and teams of convicts were employed in the dangerous and back-breaking work of felling these giants and transporting them back to Sarah Island.

Many convicts involved in timber-getting escaped into the bush and tried to make their way overland towards Hobart. Most of them

Matthew Brady.

were never heard of again. The most famous escape from Macquarie Island was by sea. In 1824, Matthew Brady, who four years earlier had been transported for forgery, led a group of 14 convicts who seized a boat and managed to row it out of Hell's Gates and right around the south of Van Diemen's Land to the shores of the Derwent River. For the next two years, Brady and his gang roamed the island, raiding farms and homesteads. His gang at one stage grew to about 100 members, as many assigned convicts left their masters and joined the bushrangers. Finally, in May 1826, Brady was wounded and captured near Launceston. He was hanged soon afterwards in Hobart.

A number of prisoners at Macquarie Harbour were so desperate that they murdered their guards, or even other convicts, so that they would be taken to Hobart and hanged. For them, death seemed preferable to the hell on earth of life at Macquarie Harbour.

Convicts towing Huon pine logs past Grummet Island toward Sarah Island in Van Diemen's Land.

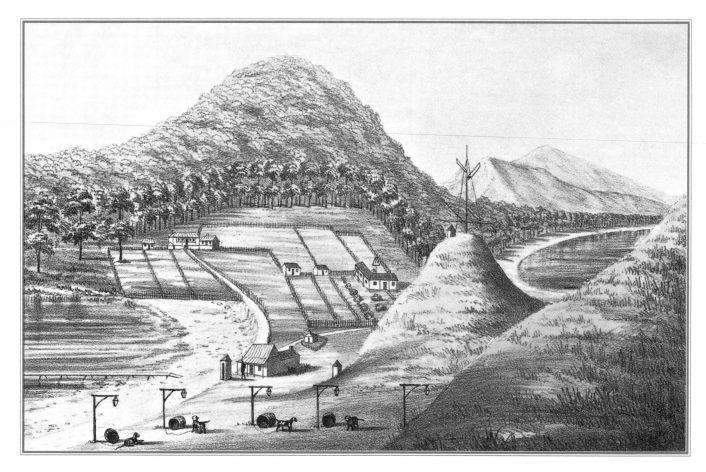

Eagle Hawk Neck at Port Arthur, with its row of guard dogs.

Port Arthur

In 1842, 18 years after Matthew Brady escaped from Macquarie Harbour, another convict bushranger, Martin Cash, made a daring escape from a penal station in Van Diemen's Land. This was the penal station at Port Arthur, situated on the Tasman Peninsula, south of Hobart. Port Arthur was opened in 1830. By this time, Macquarie Harbour, because it was so isolated, was proving too hard to maintain and to provision. George Arthur, who had replaced Sorell as Lieutenant-Governor in 1824, decided that a place closer to Hobart was required. The place he chose seemed perfect for a prison. It was separated from the rest of the island by two narrow and exposed necks of land: Eagle Hawk Neck and East Bay Neck. This made escape extremely difficult, if not almost impossible, especially as Eagle Hawk Neck was protected by a military guard, as well as by a row of guard dogs. The dogs, which were half-starved and therefore vicious, were chained to a series of posts, each of which had an oil lamp hanging from it.

The 17-year-old Martin Cash came to Sydney from Ireland in 1828, sentenced to seven years transportation for shooting and wounding another youth. After some time working as an assigned servant in the Hunter Valley, Cash was given a ticket of leave for good behaviour. In 1837, he moved to Van Diemen's Land as a free settler, where he found work on farms. In 1840 he was convicted for possession of stolen poultry and sentenced to seven years hard labour. He made two successful escapes from road gangs he was working on, but was eventually recaptured and sent to Port Arthur. Here he first tried to escape by swimming past Eagle Hawk Neck, but was again recaptured when he landed. For some reason, he was not flogged. Nor was he forced to work in chains with a heavy wooden block attached to it, which was the usual punishment for those who attempted escape.

This made it possible for him to try again. Together with two other convicts, Lawrence Kavanagh and George Jones, he escaped again in December 1842, by swimming past Eagle Hawk Neck and then managing to slip by the guards on East Bay Neck. For several months after that, Cash, Kavanagh and Jones operated as bushrangers in the area around Hobart.

A harsh regime

Prisoners at Port Arthur were subject to very harsh discipline. Floggings were frequent and solitary confinement, in tiny, cramped, dark cells for days at a time, was a dreaded punishment. Another dreaded punishment was to be sent to work in the coal mine at a place called Coal Point. The coal was not of good quality, but it could be sold in Hobart for a fraction of the cost of coal from New South Wales. Work in the coal mine was hard, dirty and dangerous.

Timber-getting was another important industy at Port Arthur. So was agriculture. Teams of convicts, sometimes chained together, pulled ploughs to turn the hard earth. Others tended orchards and cultivated crops. There was also a kind of railway at Port Arthur. It consisted of open carts, with iron wheels which ran on timber rails. Visitors to the settlement rode four to a cart, pushed, uphill and downhill, by convicts.

Convict boys

A part of Port Arthur, separated from the main convict settlement, is known as Point Puer. 'Puer' is the Latin word for 'boy', and from 1833, shiploads of convict boys, aged from 10 to 18, were sent to Point Puer. Part of the reason for setting up Point Puer was to keep the young convicts separated from the older, hardened criminals who might encourage them in crime. Another aim was to reform the boys by teaching them trades. Specially chosen boys at Point Puer were taught trades such as blacksmithing, bootmaking, baking and carpentry. Many of them ended up earning a living as free citizens from these trades. But the boys had to earn the right to learn a trade. When they arrived at Point Puer all boys were forced to work in labouring gangs, performing tasks such as clearing land, making roads and collecting firewood. Many

The convict-powered railway at Port Arthur.

Port Arthur in the 1860s. Even though transportation to Van Diemen's Land ceased in 1852, convicts continued to serve out their sentences in the penal colony.

of the more troublesome boys never graduated from these gangs to become apprentice tradesmen.

Punishments at Point Puer were severe, but not as harsh as those given to adult offenders. Canings were common, and repeated offenders were often locked up in solitary confinement and fed only bread and water for several days. Violence often broke out as boys fought with each other, or attacked their guards, who were usually convict men. In 1843, two 14-year-old boys murdered their convict overseer.

Point Puer was closed down in 1849, but adult prisoners were still kept at Port Arthur until 1877, even though transportation to Van Diemen's Land stopped in 1852. Three years after the last convicts arrived in Van Diemen's Land, the name of the colony was officially changed to Tasmania. The name Van Diemen's Land was strongly associated in people's minds with the colony's convict past. Tasmanians now wanted to look forward to a future as a free society.

Governor George Arthur.

OTHER PENAL SETTLEMENTS

After Governor Lachlan Macquarie left New South Wales in 1822, life became more difficult for convicts. The new governor, Sir Thomas Brisbane, was determined to punish convicts who repeatedly committed offences or who attempted to escape. He therefore set up a number of new settlements, which like Macquarie Harbour and Port Arthur in Van Diemen's Land, were to be places of secondary punishment.

A penal settlement had existed at Coal Harbour (which is now Newcastle), about 110 kilometres north of Sydney, since early in the 19th century. In 1801, Governor King sent a few convicts there to mine coal, but at that time Coal Harbour proved too difficult to administer from faraway Sydney and the convicts were brought back. But in March 1804, an event occurred which made King reconsider his decision.

There were at that time about 200 convicts at a farming settlement called Castle Hill, near Parramatta. The great majority of these convicts were Irish. Most of them had been transported for theft and similar crimes, but some had been sentenced because they had taken part in rebellions against the British government, which ruled Ireland. There was always strong tension between the Irish convicts and their British guards, and the authorities in New South Wales feared a revolt by the Irish convicts.

At about eight o'clock in the evening of Sunday 4 March, the Irish convicts at Castle Hill, led by Phillip Cunningham and William Johnston, suddenly set fire to one of the farm buildings and then went on a rampage. They grabbed whatever weapons they could get their hands on —including swords, axes, pitchforks, as well as some guns—and set out for Parramatta. As they went, they looted farms and attacked settlers. They went to the house of the government flogger and severely beat him. Their plan was to go on to Sydney, encouraging other Irish convicts that were assigned to farmers to join them on the way. In Sydney, they would seize some boats and escape from the colony. It was a foolhardy plan that could not succeed.

News of the uprising reached Sydney about midnight. The New South Wales Corps, under Major George Johnston, grouped together and, heavily armed, marched towards Parramatta. They met the rebels at a place called Vinegar Hill and called on them to surrender. The rebels refused, claiming they would have either 'death or liberty'. A battle broke out, and the convicts, many of whom were now thoroughly drunk, were easily overcome. About 15 convicts were shot dead, and many were wounded. Cunningham and other ringleaders were captured and Cunningham, who was also wounded, was hanged that same night, without a trial.

The punishment for the other leaders was terrible. Eight of them were hanged in chains and their bodies left to rot in public. Nine others were publicly and viciously flogged. Others involved in the riot were put in irons and made to work in road gangs. King decided that another 35 would be sent to Coal Harbour to reopen the settlement and mine the coal there. King renamed the settlement Newcastle, and it became the first place of secondary punishment in the colony.

Newcastle, like other, later penal settlements, became a place of dread for the convicts. Convicts, often underfed and with their clothes in rags, were employed for up to 12 hours a day in the filthy and arduous work of mining coal, or in the equally hard and dangerous work of timber-getting. But the most dreaded work was at the limeburners' camp, about 10 kilometres from the main settlement. Here men collected oyster shells from the beaches and from the riverbed and then burnt them in kilns to produce lime. This lime would be taken to Sydney to produce mortar for buildings. The lime burnt the convicts' skin and stung their eyes. Some deliberately blinded themselves to try and get out of this work.

An early painting, depicting the clash between soldiers and rebel convicts at Vinegar Hill.

Settlements further north

By the early 1820s, Newcastle was no longer an isolated settlement. Free settlers had moved onto the land near the Hunter River and most of the cedar forests had been logged. In 1823 Newcastle was declared a 'free town' and most of the convicts there were transferred to a new penal colony about 300 kilometres further north on the coast at Port Macquarie. Some convicts stayed on at Newcastle, mainly to work in the coal mines, but it was no longer a place only for repeat offenders.

In 1824, the year after convicts had been moved to Port Macquarie, Governor Brisbane decided to create yet another penal settlement, this time much further north on the Brisbane River, near the site of present-day Brisbane. The new penal colony was known as Moreton Bay. One reason for choosing this location was the large numbers of convicts who managed to escape into the bush at Port Macquarie. Moreton Bay was so far north of any other settlement that it would be impossible to escape and survive. In fact, there were many escape attempts at Moreton Bay. In the late 1820s, when there were about 1200 convicts at Moreton Bay, almost one-tenth of them headed south into the bush. More than half the escapees eventually found their weary way back to the settlement, where they were ruthlessly flogged and made to work in irons. The rest were never seen again.

Life for convicts at both Port Macquarie and Moreton Bay was similar in many ways to the life the convicts at Newcastle had endured. At Moreton Bay, particularly, punishments for even minor offences were extremely severe. Moreton Bay was so far from the main settlement at Sydney that the commandant of the penal colony could act very much as he wished. One of the most hated of all penal colony commandants was Captain Patrick Logan, who was in charge of Moreton Bay between 1826 and 1830. Logan was speared to death by Aborigines in 1830, while he was out exploring the surrounding countryside. When news of his death reached the convicts, there was wild rejoicing.

Newcastle in 1825, just after it ceased being a place of secondary punishment.

Norfolk Island

You read on pages 36–8 about the convict settlement that existed on Norfolk Island between 1788 and 1814. In 1825, Governor Brisbane ordered that a new penal settlement be set up on Norfolk Island. The free settlers who had arrived there since 1814 were to be moved to a new settlement near Hobart in Van Diemen's Land, known as New Norfolk. The Norfolk Island settlement was deliberately designed to be a place where convicts would endure terrible punishments. Brisbane wrote of the penal settlements in 1825 that convicts should be sent to Port Macquarie for the 'first grave offences'; they should be sent to Moreton Bay if they escaped from Port Macquarie; and Norfolk Island was to be the 'ne plus ultra' (a Latin term which meant that Norfolk Island was to be the worst imaginable place of punishment). 'Felons on Norfolk Island,' he wrote, 'have forfeited all claim to the protection of the law.' Two years later, Brisbane's successor, Governor Ralph Darling, wrote that he intended to make Norfolk Island 'a place of extremest Punishment, short of Death'.

For almost 30 years, Norfolk Island was a place of misery for most of the men sent there. (No women convicts were sent to Norfolk Island during this period.) Some of them chose death rather than life on the island. Suicides were common and convicts often committed murder so that they could be transported back to Sydney and hanged. Some even imagined that they might be able to escape while being taken back to Sydney for trial. In 1833, however, a new law allowed trials and hangings to take place on the island and this slim hope of escape was therefore cut off.

There were two major uprisings on Norfolk Island. In 1834, a mob of about 200 convicts tried to take over the island and escape by ship. Like the earlier uprising at Castle Hill, this one was

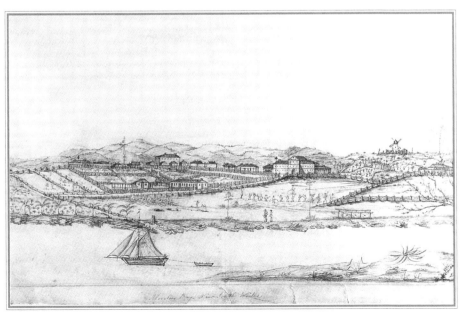

The penal colony at Moreton Bay in 1835.

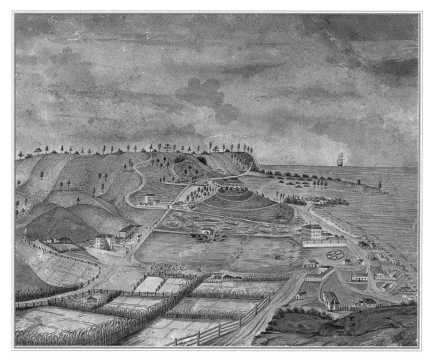

The penal colony at Kingston on Norfolk Island in 1835. The convict barracks and gaol is the three-storey building near the shore.

poorly planned and was easily put down by the soldiers. While awaiting trial, the ringleaders were repeatedly flogged and tortured in other ways. Eventually, months later, 30 convicts were condemned to death, but 16 of these had their sentences commuted to hard labour for life. The other fourteen were hanged on the island in September 1834.

In July 1846, a riot broke out when convicts, who were very poorly fed, discovered that some food supplies that they had stolen and hidden had been found and removed by the authorities. The rioters stormed towards the storeroom to recover their provisions, killing four guards on their way. The rioters, however, were soon herded into the prison's lumberyard and subdued. Twelve of the leaders of the revolt were sentenced to death and were hanged, in two groups of six, on 13 October 1846.

One of the men who died for his part in this revolt was Lawrence Kavanagh. He was one of the men who escaped from Port Arthur in 1842 with Martin Cash. You read about that escape on pages 52–3. Both Cash and Kavanagh were captured some months after making their escape, and both of them ended up being sent to Norfolk Island as hard-core criminals.

Most of the convicts on Norfolk Island had been involved in this riot. One of the few who played no part in it was Martin Cash. Cash, it

seemed, had learned the error of his ways and had behaved well on Norfolk Island. He was treated more leniently than most other prisoners, was given an easy job in the prison bakehouse and in 1853 was pardoned and freed. After his release, he went back to Tasmania. Some years later he purchased a farm near Hobart and lived there until he died in 1877, at the age of 67. At least in the last 20 years of his life, Martin Cash can be considered one of the success stories of the convict era.

The bushranger Martin Cash, photographed after his release from Norfolk Island.

FEMALE FACTORIES

One of the last buildings that Francis Greenway designed for Governor Macquarie is no longer standing today. It was a new 'female factory' at Parramatta. This building was constructed to replace a previous female factory that had been established above the main prison at Parramatta in 1804.

The female factory at Parramatta was one of several similar institutions for women convicts that existed in the colonies. You read earlier how many women convicts were 'assigned' to act as servants and workers on farms and in private households. Many others married or lived with male convicts, army officers, soldiers or free settlers. Those who remained single, who refused to work or who for some other reason could not be assigned were sent to these female factories. Convict women who committed crimes after arriving in the colony were also sent to the female factories as punishment. Single women who were pregnant, or who had nowhere else to care for their children, were also housed in the female factories. Often women who became pregnant while they were assigned as servants were sent to the female factory, because the families they worked for did not want the responsibility of having a baby in their house. Women in the female factories worked at various jobs— mainly spinning and weaving cloth and making clothes.

The female factories, then, were a combination of workhouse, prison, hospital and nursery. They were often unpleasant, overcrowded and unruly places. As early as 1812, Governor Macquarie had written to the British government, asking permission to build a new female factory to replace the one above the Parramatta gaol. It was not until 1816 that he received permission to proceed. There was no doubt that a new building was needed. At the end of 1817, for example, Macquarie admitted that there were 200 women in a building that was fit to house only about 60. When Commissioner Bigge arrived in 1819,

Greenway's new building was already under construction, but Bigge still made an inspection of the old 'factory'. He described the 'offensive' drains, the dirty walls, the unsatisfactory bedding and the inadequate discipline. He found the place, he said, in a 'state of disgusting filth' and the appearance of the women to be 'disordered, unruly and licentious'. Another criticism was that the women who had been sent to the factory for committing crimes in the colony were treated exactly the same as the other women there. They were not forced to do more work and they were given the same rations.

The new factory at Parramatta

Conditions in the new factory were certainly much better. When it was completed, Macquarie described it as a 'large . . . handsome stone-built barrack and factory three stories high with wings of one story each for the accommodation . . . of three hundred female convicts'. The work rooms included 'weaving and loom rooms, work shops, stores for wool, flax etc.' The grounds covered an area of about 4 acres (1.6 hectares) and were surrounded by a 'high stone wall or wet ditch'. On 1 February 1821, 100 women and 71 children were moved into the new factory. Forty of the women were there because they had committed crimes in the colony.

Macquarie drew up a set of rules for the new female factory. These were intended to improve discipline and behaviour. After six months good behaviour, a woman could go into a special 'class' called the 'first' or 'merit' class. These women were allowed to work part of the time for pay. After 12 months in the merit class, a woman was allowed to go and work outside the factory, or to get married if anyone wanted to marry her. They were also allowed to leave the factory for short periods. Free settlers and emancipists would frequently visit the female factory to choose a wife from the eligible women. Women who behaved

The female factory that opened at Parramatta in 1821.

badly were placed in a 'crime' or 'third' class and were forced to do hard manual labour such as breaking up stones.

Within the factory, women had to wear a special uniform. They wore a different uniform on Sundays. Women in the crime class were forced to wear a badge as a form of public disgrace. Women who repeatedly misbehaved were placed in solitary confinement in tiny cells. The punishment that the women dreaded most was having their head shaved. These women were treated as objects of ridicule both by the guards and by many of the other convict women.

Like the old factory, the new factory eventually became dirty and overcrowded and the discipline worsened. Riots and even attempts to burn the building down were not uncommon. In 1827, for example, about 100 women escaped from the factory when their rations were reduced. They went into the town of Parramatta, stealing food from residents. Some of them headed off into the bush and were not rounded up for several days.

In February 1831, the women objected to the strictness of one of their overseers. They grabbed her and shaved her head, then broke out and headed for Parramatta. They were stopped by soldiers on the way and forced back into the factory. Often, when unruly behaviour broke out, soldiers were called in to prevent a violent riot.

The female factory at Parramatta was closed down in 1842, two years after the transportation of convicts to New South Wales ended.

Other female factories

If conditions in the Parramatta female factory were bad, those in the one that opened in 1829 at Cascades, near Hobart in Van Diemen's Land, were worse. As at Parramatta, women here were put into 'classes'. Babies who were born at Cascades were taken away from their convict mothers when they were nine months old and the mothers were then put into the third, or criminal class, as a punishment for becoming pregnant. The unfortunate mothers had already been punished by having their food

The female factory at Cascades in Van Diemen's Land.

about the plight of the women convicts and conditions became almost as bad as before.

Other, smaller, female factories existed for some time at the penal settlements of Port Macquarie and Moreton Bay. Only very few women were sent to these settlements, which were established as places of punishment for convicts who had committed crimes after arriving in the colony. Between 1824 and 1839, only about 150 women went to Moreton Bay. The female factory at Port Macquarie housed an average of between 20 and 30 women at any one time.

rations reduced after their babies were born. This was the time, while they were feeding their infants, that they most needed reasonable food! As a result, many newborn babies, and some mothers, died from malnutrition.

Even without the reduced rations, many babies at Cascades would have died as a result of the damp and filthy conditions. Between January and March 1838, for example, 20 people died in the factory—most of them babies. A jury investigated the situation and found that up to 70 mothers and infants were confined in two small, narrow rooms, 8 metres long and 3.5 metres wide. A terrible stench filled these rooms. Outside was a damp exercise yard, which received no sunlight for at least four months of every year. The tiny, dark cells where some women spent up to a month in solitary confinement, existing only on bread and water, were described as 'extremely offensive'. Overall, the jury found, the Cascades factory was 'wholly unfit and unsuited for the punishment of the females'.

The results of this inquiry received some publicity, and for a while things improved slightly. The dark solitary confinement rooms were closed—but only for a short time—and the nursery was moved out of the factory to cleaner, healthier premises. However, people soon forgot

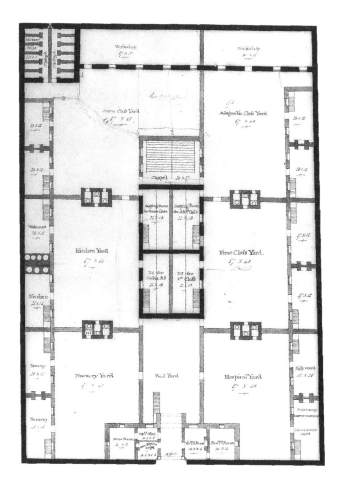

These plans for the Cascades female factory were drawn up in 1827.

AN END AND A NEW BEGINNING

In 1840, the British government decided to end the transportation of convicts to New South Wales. Opposition to transportation increased in the Australian colonies as the number of free settlers and emancipists grew. Even large landholders, who had benefited by being able to employ convict workers for very little pay, were against it. They could now employ newly arrived free immigrants at very little cost. By the late 1830s, only a few wealthy settlers still argued in favour of continued transportation. There was also strong opposition in Britain. Influential people there argued that transportation was not really a punishment at all. They pointed out that many convicts had ended up as rich and comfortable free citizens. Others spent their whole sentences in easy jobs as assigned servants or farm workers. Also, there was now less need to send convicted criminals out of England, as new and larger prisons had been built there. The high cost of sending convicts to the other side of the world was another important factor.

In 1839 a new system of treating convicts began in Van Diemen's Land. Convicts were no longer assigned to work for settlers. Under this system, which was called the 'probation' system, all convicts would work for the government in work gangs. They did hard physical work, such as making roads and working on public buildings. After two years, if they kept out of trouble and worked well, they were given a 'probation pass' and were permitted to work for wages. After some time, convicts with probation passes could get a ticket of leave. Those convicted of crimes while in the colony could be sent to the penal colony at Port Arthur or to Norfolk Island. The system, which was supposed to ensure that convicts were punished for their crimes as well as being rewarded for hard work and good behaviour, did not work well. For one thing, there was not enough public work to keep the convicts in the gangs busy. For another, those convicts with probation passes or tickets of leave found it increasingly difficult to find paid jobs. A lot of these convicts turned to crime in order to make a living.

The situation became desperate, especially when ex-convicts from Van Diemen's Land began to pour into Victoria as the gold rushes began in 1851. Anti-Transportation Leagues formed in Sydney, Melbourne and Hobart and there were huge public meetings. Some speakers at these demonstrations even suggested that the colonies should declare themselves independent of Britain if any more convicts were sent. Mainly as a result of this agitation, the British government decided in 1852 to send no more convicts to the eastern Australian colonies.

Convicts in the west

John Frederick Mortlock's story is an unusual one. He was transported, not once, but twice to the Australian colonies. In 1843, he was convicted of shooting and injuring his uncle during an argument about money. He was sentenced to transportation for 21 years and went first to Norfolk Island and then to Van Diemen's Land. In 1852 he was granted a ticket of leave and spent the next five years travelling and working in different parts of Van Diemen's Land (which was renamed Tasmania in 1855) and New South Wales. In 1857, he made the mistake of sailing back to England to claim some money he had inherited. As he was a ticket of leave holder, he was still considered a convict. For a convict to return to England before his sentence was completed was a crime. Almost as soon as he arrived in England, Mortlock was arrested. He was sentenced to spend a year in prison and then to be transported for five years—not to New South Wales or Tasmania, but to the Swan River settlement (now Perth) in Western Australia. In 1865, when his sentence had expired, he once again sailed, this time legally, back to England.

As in Adelaide, the first European settlers in Western Australia were free immigrants. They arrived in 1829. But things did not go well for the new colony. Crops proved hard to grow and new immigrants difficult to attract. In 1832, only three years after the colony was founded, only 1500 of the original 4000 settlers remained. By 1849, the white population had risen to only 4500. This was not enough to keep the settlement going. There were simply not enough workers to maintain a town or to farm the land. The settlers asked the British government to send convicts, and it agreed. Between 1850 and 1868, about 10 000 male convicts were sent to Western Australia. To ensure that the population remained balanced, the government also sent about the same number of free settlers. By 1868 the population of the colony had risen to 24 000.

Convicts in Western Australia were generally treated less harshly than those in the eastern colonies. They were sometimes flogged, but only if they committed crimes of violence. Most convicts, too, were granted pardons before the end of their sentences. All were employed by the government on public works, such as roads and public buildings. One of these buildings was the prison building in Fremantle, which housed the most troublesome convicts. The main cell block could hold up to 1000 prisoners. These buildings continued to be used as a prison until 1991.

Convicts working in the grounds of Government House, Perth, in the 1860s.

(They are now an historical museum.) The convicts in the Fremantle prison worked in chain gangs, but most convict gangs in Western Australia were not made to wear chains.

During the 1860s people in the eastern colonies became alarmed at the number of ex-convicts from Western Australia who found their way eastwards. South Australian and Victorian governments even passed laws forbidding ex-convicts to go to those colonies. They were, of course, impossible to enforce. In any case, by this time the British government was running out of convicts to send. The crime rate in England, and especially in Ireland, had declined dramatically. Therefore, it decided to end transportation.

The last convict ship to Western Australia, and to anywhere in the Australian colonies, arrived in Fremantle Harbour in January 1868. Without convicts the colony of Western Australia would not have survived. By 1868, it was on its way to prosperity.

The port of Fremantle soon after the end of the convict era.

INDEX